NUCLEAR VERDICTS

VERDICTS

DEFENDING JUSTICE FOR ALL

NUCLEAR
VERDICTS

DEFENDING JUSTICE FOR ALL

ROBERT F. TYSON, JR.

LAW DOG
PUBLISHING LLC

Published by Law Dog Publishing, LLC.

Copyright © 2020 by Robert F. Tyson, Jr.

First Edition

Law Dog Publishing, LLC.
5661 La Jolla Blvd.
La Jolla, CA 92037

Cover Design by Kira Giannoni
Cover Layout & Interior Design: GKS Creative, www.gkscreative.com

Nuclear Verdict is a book of general information and should not be
interpreted as legal advice.

Contributing Publications

Personalizing the Corporate Defendant by Emily Straub
Accept Responsibility for Something by Kyle Pederson
Defuse Anger & Avoid Runaway Jury Verdicts by Pari Granum
Always Give a Number, Always! by Kate Besch
Paving the Road to Recovery – The Good News by Jessica Heppenstall
Bigger Values Work by Reece Roman
Argue Pain & Suffering by Kelly Denham
Silent Witnesses Often Testify the Loudest by Morgan Van Buren

Library of Congress Case Number: 1-8299513821

ISBN: 978-1-948792-02-8 (Hardcover)
ISBN: 978-1-948792-03-5 (Paperback)
ISBN: 978-1-948792-04-2 (eBook)

For media or booking inquiries, please contact:

STRATEGIES Public Relations
P.O. Box 178122
San Diego, CA 92177
760-550-9850
jkuritz@strategiespr.com

First printed in the United State of America.

This book is dedicated to ...

My Family

TABLE OF CONTENTS

INTRODUCTION

JUSTICE FOR ALL!

IT IS TIME TO take back justice. It has been hijacked. Runaway jury verdicts are all too common in America. Outrageous, "nuclear verdicts," based on fear and emotion, not evidence or the law, must be stopped. And YOU are going to stop it!

This book will teach you specific methods to eliminate large, unsubstantiated jury verdicts. You will learn how to develop, present, and ultimately argue damages to a jury. This book will show insurance companies, businesses, corporate counsel, governments, and defense lawyers how to control and limit damages. There are at least ten things defense attorneys must do to avoid exposing their clients to excessive damage awards. In fact, if you research large jury verdicts, you will find defense counsel almost always failed to do at least one, if not all, of these ten things.

The good news is all defense counsel and their clients can implement these methods to achieve justice. It's not difficult to do. You have to read this book, question these ten core principles— because they are not intuitive or comfortable— ultimately believe in them. Unfortunately, too few clients and their defense counsel are willing to try these methods and ultimately fall victim to manipulative, creative, and sometimes even brilliant plaintiff's lawyers.

THE SOLUTION IS YOU

YOU are the answer to the problem of nuclear verdicts. You do not have to write your congressman about tort reform or even run for office. You do not have to fix a broken system. The jury system in America is not broken. It is the greatest legal system in the world, and it works! No, YOU are the answer to large jury verdicts, but you must do more. This book will tell you exactly what more must be done.

A lot of people think the jury system is out of control. They will refer to the McDonald's hot cup of coffee case where the scalded plaintiff got tons of money for getting exactly what she ordered, hot coffee! Or Hulk Hogan getting over $100 million for damage to his reputation for a sex tape. Hulk Hogan's reputation was what exactly before it was "damaged" by his own sex tape? He is a retired wrestler famous for self-promotion and leaping around wrestling rings in tights. $100 million to restore his reputation to what?

Any lawsuit where people fail to take personal responsibility for their actions and are still awarded millions of dollars by a jury form the basis of many peoples' belief the jury system is broken.

IF IT ISN'T BROKEN...

Do unusual or unexpected outcomes mean a system is broken? Is the legal system the only place where perceived unfair results occur? Ask the same people who believe the jury system is broken whether anything good has ever happened to them at work or in business. Have they ever gotten a good deal on something? Suppose one of these folks were able to get a great price on a piece of real estate. Maybe they bought it out of foreclosure. Maybe they bought it from a little old lady, or a developer down on his luck, or maybe they just understood the value of the deal better. Whatever the reason, just because one side got a better deal on real estate than the other doesn't mean the whole real estate system in America is broken. Does anyone push for "real estate reform"? Does anyone talk at cocktail parties about realtors being the problem with America? No!

So if the legal system is not broken, then why are there so many unexplainable jury verdicts? First of all, it goes both ways. There are unimaginable defense verdicts and there are unfathomable multimillion-dollar jury verdicts. The only difference is the big jury awards make the news. Small verdicts or defense verdicts rarely get any publicity. The biggest wins of my career, such as defense verdicts or jury awards that were many millions of dollars less than what we offered in settlement, never make the news. A big win for either side doesn't always mean justice. So why does it happen?

BATTLE FOR JUSTICE

Let's be clear right up front: injured people should be compensated. They should receive fair and reasonable compensation from the party who caused them harm. Our judicial system generally does a remarkable job of ensuring justice is served upon those who deserve it. This book is not about those instances. This book is about fighting individuals and groups who are attempting to take advantage of our legal system. There are people every day who make false and exaggerated claims in the hope of receiving a windfall of cash. Many of these folks are doing it under the thinly veiled claim of justice. Claiming to have a mild traumatic brain injury that will require millions of dollars in future care, when you're not truly injured— is not justice. Claiming complex regional pain disorder or fibromyalgia or post-traumatic stress syndrome or TMJ or any other catch-all personal injury claim that's in fashion— is not justice. Claiming you were wrongfully terminated when you know you were not doing your job, or trying to anger a jury about issues that have nothing to do with the facts of a case, is not justice. These ploys and tactics must be stopped and this book will help you do it.

You are on the right side of this battle. Opportunistic plaintiff's counsel regularly attempt to villainize the defense. They will reference the big, bad, greedy insurance companies. Or careless corporate America that cares only about profits. Or the defense lawyers who work up their cases only for the billable hours. But without you on that wall, fighting for fairness, there would be no justice.

You (or your clients) have created something of value, something worth protecting. You are a business owner helping the community, or a corporation that has changed the world for the better, or a professional who has studied and learned his trade for many years and is giving sound advice every day. Your life should not be ruined or your company bankrupted because of emotional pleas or psychological tricks by unscrupulous lawyers. That is not justice.

The good news? This book will give you the tools to eliminate one of the main causes of nuclear jury verdicts. If you follow the steps outlined here, you and your counsel will not get out-lawyered!

WHY DO WE HAVE CRAZY JURY VERDICTS?
I believe there are typically two reasons for outrageous jury verdicts. The first is greed. The second is bad lawyering.

Greed is not good, at least not in front of juries. A greedy lawyer will get slaughtered. And it goes both ways. A defense lawyer who goes for a defense verdict in the face of all odds and jury research, or gives the jury no defense damages number to consider, may learn a very difficult lesson.

For the plaintiff's lawyer, greed is also often a death knell. Greed for plaintiff's attorneys rears its head when they ask the jury for too much money. Or when they stretch their claims beyond what is real and verifiable. Like adding a traumatic brain injury claim to what would have been a sizable orthopedic surgery case. A serious spinal surgery case will get a substantial jury verdict. But when you try to recover more nebulous claims on top of it, a jury may discount it all, giving a lesser verdict than if plaintiff's counsel had only presented the objectively viable claim. Neither of these two scenarios are fair to plaintiff or defendant, but the result comes from greed. Greed is not good, for either side.

PLAINTIFF'S LAWYERS ARE GOOD!

The second reason for unthinkable jury verdicts, bad lawyering, is much more common. One side or the other is surprised, or unprepared, or just not as good as the other. For nuclear jury verdicts, this usually means the plaintiff's lawyer was a lot better. And they are. Many plaintiff's lawyers study psychology, they study their trade more, they experiment, they push the envelope in trial and come up with novel damages arguments. Would a defense lawyer ever dress up in a full chicken suit to give a closing argument? Not likely. But an extremely creative and effective plaintiff's lawyer did recently in Los Angeles and the jury awarded over $20 million!

DEFENSE LAWYERS ARE VICTIMS

Do plaintiff's lawyers have the upper hand on creativity? Does the law favor allowing plaintiff's counsel more leeway in arguing damages? Do judges allow plaintiff's lawyers to "get away with" more than defense counsel? Do plaintiff's attorneys have a "better story" than the defense because they represent someone who has been injured or terminated from their job or wronged in some way? Do plaintiff's attorneys have the upper hand on justice?

If you answered yes to any of these questions, you are wrong. But you are not alone.

Almost all defense lawyers are rule followers. There is nothing wrong with that. Being defense lawyers suits us. There is comfort in knowing the parameters and staying within them. It can give you comfort in an otherwise extremely adversarial profession. Follow the rules and everything will be okay.

But this is no longer true. Times have changed. Follow the rules, follow the herd, and sometimes you will get led off a cliff to your death. Defense counsel gripes about the antics of plaintiff's counsel all the time. Defense lawyers complain to each other during trial that they cannot believe what the plaintiff's lawyers just did or tried to do. We can't believe the trial judge "allowed" plaintiff's counsel to argue something or get in certain evidence.

The solution? Get over it and win already!

Don't be a victim!

GET IN THE GAME!

Trial is like many things we have do in our everyday lives. It's like an athletic competition or a complex board game, such as chess, or any number of rule-based activities. I sometimes analogize trial to a basketball game. If you ever played basketball, think about when you were lining up for the jump ball to start the game. You are standing next to your opponent, both of you wearing shiny short shorts with white cotton wristbands and headbands, and socks pulled up to your knees. (OK, forget that last part; that was me growing up in New York in the '70s.) As you're standing there waiting for the game to begin and the ball to be tipped your way, what are you thinking about? Are you thinking, "Boy, I sure hope I don't get any fouls in this game." No way! You're thinking, "I want to win!"

Trial is the same thing. It's a competition. There are winners and losers. You must want to win! And like basketball, the winner is not the side who gets the least fouls. Basketball has referees to enforce the rules, maybe a little like a judge. You get a certain number of fouls every game before you are out of the game, typically five. You get "fouls" in a trial, too. It's when the other side objects and the judge sustains the objection. For instance, you asked an objectionable question or tried to get some document or fact into evidence but the judge ruled against you. You essentially got called for a foul.

Use your fouls! Defense lawyers are afraid to foul. We would much rather complain about the plaintiff "fouling" all the time or how the referee is not being fair to both sides. Use your fouls! Don't "foul out" of a trial, of course. Don't get an intentional foul or a flagrant foul. You never want to get sanctioned or be held in contempt or even get admonished in front of the jury. But getting an honest foul, when you're trying to get to the truth, is part of a trial.

Do you know who uses all of their fouls? That's right, plaintiff's counsel! The best plaintiff's lawyers in the country are always, and I mean always, pushing the envelope. They do so because they are advocating for their client or, as they would claim, they are fighting for justice. Aren't you, though? Aren't you fighting for justice too? Do you not want the best outcome possible? Do you not want truth and justice to prevail above all else? Of course you do! The way we do that is to fight for justice and fight to win, just like the other side does.

THE PLAYBOOK

This book will show you how to combat the tactics plaintiff's counsel is using to obtain outrageous jury verdicts. You will learn how to be ready for their intentional "fouls" that are written about in many of their books and other publications.

And why are there so many more books written for plaintiff's lawyers than defense lawyers? Why are plaintiff's attorneys so much more connected with each other than defense counsel? They watch each other in trial. They help each other. They share information. They know more about me and my firm than I can ever imagine. And it is all very effective for them.

The defense? We share very little. Each defense firm, and often each defense lawyer, is his own separate island. We are left to learn on our own. To learn in the trenches against the best plaintiff's lawyers in the country. Oh, we have wonderful defense organizations that do a tremendous amount of good and are an outstanding resource. We may work in big firms with other defense lawyers who have been to trial before. But nothing we do can compare to the plaintiff's bar.

Why are defense lawyers not more open and connected with each other? Why is this the first book written on how to argue damages from a defense perspective? Why doesn't the defense share all of these ideas with each other? There could be a few reasons, but the obvious one is, we all want the same clients! I want the business of every general counsel or risk manager or insurance person who reads this book. And if I give my "secrets" away, my competition will get these clients! Just ask my partners if they think this is a real fear!

Our business is a repeat business. If we get one insurance client or large corporation as a client, we can make a career out of it. The plaintiff's bar? It's almost always one-offs. If they do a great job for an injured plaintiff, they are not going to get thirty new files from that person a month, let alone in a lifetime! By having wide-open communication, plaintiff's counsel have almost no risk of losing any clients. In fact, their "competitors" are likely to send them their tougher cases or associate them in for trial. Me? I am not banking on my fellow defense counsel sending me any insurance clients!

So why share these secrets with my competition? Why give the other team our playbook? Literally let the plaintiff's bar know step-by-step what we are going to do to reach a fair and reasonable jury verdict. How we intend to fight them every step of the way. Why? Because this is not a game. Justice should not be about who has the better or slicker lawyer. An injured plaintiff should not get millions of dollars just because her attorney got the jury angry or made an emotional plea for sympathy. A plaintiff also should not get undercompensated just because her lawyer got greedy by adding unsubstantiated damage claims or otherwise overreaching.

Sometimes, for me, there is something more important than having a successful law practice. More important than even winning, which is pretty darn important to me. That something is fairness. I am sharing these somewhat controversial techniques because reaching a fair result is more important than winning. Our jury system is bigger than me, or the plaintiff's bar, or the judiciary. It is the cornerstone of fairness in our country. This book is intended to even the scales of justice, so that justice will be served. And if that means some plaintiff's lawyers will become even better prepared to game the system after reading this book, then I will take that chance to ensure all defendants are afforded the protections of our Constitution.

SHADOWS IN THE DARK

Being a trial lawyer is a tough job. It's hard for both sides. It's a battle. You feel as if you are at odds with everyone. The plaintiff's attorneys, who I do admire and respect, often only get paid if they win. That pressure is tremendous and should never be underestimated. I live in fear. Fear of losing, or what twelve strangers are going to think of me or my case. There is plenty to feel insecure about as a trial lawyer. And the day you aren't worried about losing, could very well be the day you do!

Trial lawyers make many sacrifices. We spend a considerable amount of time away from our families. We often stare at the popcorn ceilings of rundown motel rooms that happen to be within walking distance of faraway courthouses.

I still see the dark shadow of my young son waving to me from his bedroom window as I was getting in a van for an early morning flight to an out-of-town trial. It was awful, heart wrenching. As I rubbed away my tears, there was nothing I wanted to do more than go back into my house and lay in bed with him. He was only awake in the darkness of the morning because he heard me, heard my luggage wheeling out the door, again. He was only waving to me because he missed me and wanted me to stay home.

So why ever leave the silhouette in the window of my beautiful son longingly waving good-bye, when it would be so easy to walk back into the house to my loving wife and two other daughters? What makes one routinely confront their own fears and insecurities? The answer is not always crystal clear or easy to remember in these lonely moments. But upon reflection, sometimes there is something in the world more important than you. Something that is bigger than just you or what you want at a particular moment in time. In the case of a trial attorney, that something is truth and justice.

GET ANGRY!

So how do you fight injustice? How do you prevent nuclear jury verdicts? First of all, YOU need to get angry! You need to stop complaining and do something about it. Just like plaintiff's counsel across the country are trying to get juries angry against defendants, you need to get angry about what is being done to the jury system in America. This book is going to give you the tools to combat the latest techniques being used to obtain outrageous jury awards. But you need to find your own motivation.

What is it? Fear? Fear of losing? Fear of trying something new? Fear of defending a client or insured in a way you have never done before? Fear of taking a chance that the business-as-usual defense approach just does not work anymore? Fear of winning?

Maybe your motivation is the pursuit of justice. Maybe you are a rule follower. If you are, you should be fed up. You should be repulsed by any plaintiff's counsel who bends or breaks the rules in the pursuit of money, under the guise of pursuing justice. It affronts your sense of justice, and it should!

JUST DO IT!

So let's get going! You are going to have do some things you have never done before. You are going to have to ask some tough questions. Like, what is the theme of your case? Or how much are you going to ask the jury to award in damages, even if you're seeking a defense verdict? What are you going to accept responsibility for in this trial, even though you think you did nothing wrong? What is the good news? Has anything positive come out of this whole lawsuit? How are you going to argue pain and suffering, or emotional distress? Or most important who is the client? What is their story? I have heard plaintiffs' stories for the last several years, but what about the defendant?

Again, this book will discuss at least ten concepts that must be learned and used to avoid nuclear jury verdicts. Of course these methods are in addition to the typical defense approach of punching holes in a plaintiff's case. That must always be done. But if you're also able to adopt these techniques, I promise they will give you solace. As you wait in the hallway outside the courtroom for the jury to return a verdict, you will know that you and your attorneys have done everything you could to restore justice to our jury system. YOU are the solution to what has been wrong with our legal system. YOU will have taken back justice, ***justice for all!***

CHAPTER ONE
MR. HOWELL

THE MOMENT

"ENJOY THE MOMENT, DUDE!" That was the advice my law partner Pat Mendes gave me when I went to the California Supreme Court for the first time. I was there to argue the biggest damages case ever. There was a lot on the line that sunny morning in San Francisco. Although I was just a simple trial lawyer, not an appellate lawyer, I did try to enjoy the moment.

The California Supreme Court is no typical courthouse. The courtroom is enormous, more like a university lecture hall. The ceilings are at least three stories high and the bench for the seven justices seems to be about ten feet in the air. Behind the bench is a painted mural. It is almost as big as my house. It features colorful trees, creeks, rolling hills, and gentle billowing clouds floating across the soft blue sky. A real California landscape. The creeks were no doubt fed from the eastern Sierra Nevada mountains in the background. *Where do those streams lead,* I wondered? Somewhere peaceful and safe I was sure. What a great idea, to have such a tranquil painting to help relax attorneys before the justices take the bench. Relaxing, enjoying the moment, that's what I was doing.

Wait, why are my hands shaking? Man, my mouth sure is getting dry. I could use some water. And why are all these people here? Why is every seat in this huge courtroom taken, with observers standing several people deep in the back and lining the side aisles?

And all eyes seem to be on me. I have to go first? Why do I have to argue first—in front of all of these people—not to mention the soon-to-be arriving seven justices who will literally be looking down their noses at me?

$10 BILLION A YEAR LOSER!

Oh, that's right, I go first because for the last two years I have been a multibillion-dollar loser! I lost to the mighty Consumer Attorneys of California, the most powerful organization of plaintiff's attorneys in the country. Not only did I lose a multibillion-dollar case at the lower courts, but the Consumer Attorneys of California wanted to make sure it stayed that way. They had brought in the big guns for this fight. All new counsel had shown up at court that day. A Supreme Court "specialist." This guy seemed good, too. He wore a tailored dark suit. Although short and stout in stature, he had a deep, commanding voice. He'd been standing in line in front of me outside the courtroom, telling all who would listen why he was there, in a very confident voice that was difficult to ignore.

And now, all of these people were here to see if I was going to go down in flames as the biggest loser of all time, at the highest court of our state. Only $10 billion a year or more, every year, was on the line. There were over twenty amicus briefs filed with the court by interested companies and organizations. These "friends of the court" legal briefs were filed by all types of businesses and associations. They included AARP, the American Insurance Association, the League of California Cities, the California Medical Association; just about every major insurance company in America either filed an amicus brief or were part of an organization that did. And win or lose, my name was going to be attached to this Supreme Court decision. Sure, it would be taught in law schools one day and debated across the country, but for now, I was about to argue the biggest damages case ever in California and I was not enjoying the moment! Thanks for that advice, partner!

BILLED VS. PAID

The case was *Howell v. Hamilton Meats*. Technically, the issue the court would decide that day was whether an injured plaintiff who files a lawsuit may recover the full amount of their medical bills or the much lower amount that is actually paid by a health insurance company. Certainly not a juicy issue. Not one for which you would expect a packed courtroom. But this was about real money. Real money to injured plaintiffs, to defendants and their insurance companies, and certainly to the plaintiff's bar who was pushing this issue.

If you have ever seen a medical bill, then you know that what a hospital or other healthcare provider charges is a lot more than what is actually paid—$100 for bandages, $20 for an aspirin. The abuses have been widely reported. For instance, a hospital stay might be billed at $100,000, but what the hospital accepts as payment from your health insurer is much lower, maybe only $20,000. This $80,000 difference between what is billed and what is paid is what we were fighting over. This difference, when multiplied by the number of claims in California each year, is how you get to over $10 billion every year. And plaintiff's attorneys, who are compensated on a contingency fee or a percentage of the total recovery, stood to make $4 billion more every year if they won. Imagine, doing the same job you always do and wak-

3

ing up one morning to learn you are going to make billions of dollars more every year! That was the very real possibility for the Consumer Attorneys of California. Given what had preceded my oral argument, it was almost a forgone conclusion the plaintiff's attorneys would receive a tremendous windfall that day.

Well, not on my watch!

A WIN FOR CONSUMERS, NOT THEIR ATTORNEYS

What was the biggest loss of my career—okay, really any lawyer's career—became the biggest win of my life. Against all odds, and the considerable resources of the plaintiff's bar, we were able to convince the California Supreme Court that injured plaintiffs were only entitled to recover what is actually paid for medical expenses, not the much greater amount that is billed. Yes, this was a great win for insurance companies, businesses, and California governments. Yes, it was a crushing blow for the Consumer Attorneys of California who had picked this fight years earlier in hopes of a tremendous payday.

But the real winners, of course, were the actual consumers, the citizens of California. If the Supreme Court had increased plaintiffs' recoveries by over $10 billion a year, what was going to happen? Were insurance companies going to go out of business? Do you think State Farm and Allstate and Geico, or any other insurance company, were just going to pay the extra ten billion every year? Do you think the government was going to absorb the extra cost of these exorbitant bills? Do you think companies that did business in California were going to close their doors?

No, of course not! All of these entities would have passed the extra $10 billion a year on to the consumers! Every extra dime the Consumer Attorneys of California were seeking would have been paid by ordinary citizens in increased cost of goods, higher insurance premiums, and less government services or higher taxes. Yes, the Consumer Attorneys would have been $4 billion richer, but consumers would foot the bill.

Justice was served that day. Not only consumers, but for all. And that is what this book is going to help you achieve, justice for all!

WHERE THE REAL MONEY IS

So that is how I became known as Mr. Howell. Well, that's part of it. The focus of my career, and, in turn, this book, has been achieving reasonable damage awards and avoiding runaway jury verdicts. Years before I made it to the Supreme Court, I tried the *Howell* case to a jury in San Diego. The underlying case was a damages-only trial. We stipulated to almost everything. We stipulated to liability, causation, and all economic damages, including past and future medical expenses. The only issue for the jury was putting a dollar amount on past and future pain and suffering. In fact, I called no experts in the trial, no witnesses, and introduced no evidence! When it was my turn to present evidence, the defense simply rested.

How did we do? How did we avoid a runaway jury verdict against one of the best plaintiff's lawyers in the country without even putting on a case?

Well, it was not the "sit down defense" as one of my clients once questioned. No, we implemented all of the methods we are going to show you in this book. You will literally learn how to keep down damages without introducing evidence!

Many of the things I learned in the *Howell* case form the basis of how we argue damages to a jury today. And while the *Howell* case addressed billions of dollars in economic damages, this book will show you how to argue a much bigger component of damages. You will learn how to argue the biggest part of almost any large jury verdict, the non-economic damages—what is called "pain and suffering," or emotional distress. It's the part of a damages award that has no formula; there are no calculations. It's the harm to an injured plaintiff that's more of a feeling, more of a personal loss. It goes to the essence of the person. It could be their appearance, such as a scar, or burns, or disfigurement. Or it could go much deeper. It could be a change in personality, an inability to follow their passion, a loss of hope for a bright future. In a wrongful death action, it is the component of damages that addresses the loss of life, the loss of love, companionship, society, and comfort. Although there is no particular way for juries to calculate non-economic damages, this loss is real and it is recoverable under the law. It is the true unknown every time you pick a jury.

BRING ON THE PAIN AND SUFFERING

Everyone has a pretty good idea what the economic damages might be when they impanel a jury. In fact, many times the amount of economic loss a plaintiff claims, such as wage loss and medical expenses, is stipulated to by the parties.

Have you ever heard of a runaway jury verdict where the jury award was so outrageous because the jury gave the plaintiff all of her medical expenses? Can you believe the jury awarded $10 million to take care of a severely injured plaintiff who cannot care for herself, who is hospitalized for the rest of her life, and will need 24/7 care? No, of course not! Economic damages can be large, but generally they make sense to us. An innocent injured plaintiff should be made whole; they should receive money for medical treatment and lost wages.

The shake-your-head, how-could-this-have-happened jury verdicts are when non-economic damages are huge. When a jury feels sympathy or, even worse, gets angry. When a jury, even though instructed not to, lets their emotions enter deliberations. That's when a jury finds a way to make somebody pay. And not pay just medical expenses or lost wages, but pay in a big way. Pay much more money than anyone ever thought they would award when they walked into jury duty. A number that will send a message. A big number that will tell their community this isn't right, that we are not going to let corporations treat us or our neighbors this way. And how a runaway jury will send this message is through non-economic damages. And the only way a jury is ever moved to award such large sums of money is at the behest of extremely skilled plaintiff's attorneys.

Plaintiff's counsel knows this is the biggest part of any large personal injury verdict. They are constantly studying ways to obtain large verdicts. There are many books written for plaintiff's attorneys on how to argue damages. There are new theories on the psychology of jurors and how to exploit their fears, such as the reptile theory or David Ball's book on *Damages*. There are regular seminars and even camps that plaintiff's attorneys can attend to learn the latest jury trends and techniques to obtain large damages awards.

But on the defense side of damages? Almost nothing, until now.

THE DEFENSE MENTALITY

But why? Why is there so much written, tested, and taught to plaintiff's attorneys on how to obtain large jury verdicts? The reason is simple: this is how they get paid! Almost all attorneys who represent injured people are compensated by how much money they obtain. These lawyers are paid a percentage of the recovery, called a contingency fee. Most plaintiff's lawyers are paid a third or forty percent, or sometimes even more, of whatever money they recover for their clients.

Defense lawyers? Defense lawyers are paid the same amount of money if we win or lose. We are paid by the hour or a flat fee, regardless of whether the jury awards $1 million or zero. I would love to get a percentage of all the money I have saved my clients in jury verdicts! But it doesn't work that way. So what motivates a defense lawyer to not be a victim of a runaway jury?

For me, it is the fear of losing. Every case I try is life or death. I must win. There are no excuses. Fear of losing drives me in every trial. I do not subscribe to common defense sayings like, "Well the jury just didn't get it." Or, "If you try enough cases, you are going to win some and lose some." Nope, not for me. Every trial is like the March Madness basketball tournament, win or go home. I'm not going home! And neither are you if you read on.

WE ARE ABOUT TO LOSE BIG-TIME!

This brings us back to the Supreme Court, with me nervously waiting for the justices to take the bench. My associate on the *Howell* case had twice come to me after we lost this billion-dollar issue at the appellate level and asked me to give up the case. There were literally hundreds of appellate lawyers who wanted to take the lead on our Supreme Court argument. For an appellate lawyer, this could make their career.

It would have been very easy to give up our case to extremely competent appellate lawyers, some of whom had actually been to the Supreme Court before. (Side note: I did share ten minutes of my thirty-minute oral argument with appellate specialist Bob Olson of Greines, Martin, Stein & Richland LLP. Bob was invaluable and I owe him a debt of gratitude.) But if I was going down as a billion-dollar loser, I was going down on my own terms!

ONE IN A MILLION CHANCE

So what were my chances of winning? Not good! In most of the country, the law says that injured plaintiffs are entitled to recover the full amount of their medical bills. So most of the country was against me.

Then, I had already lost at the lower appellate court level two years earlier. In addition, this very same issue had been addressed by three other appellate courts at about the same time. Three out of four appellate courts, including in my case, had ruled against our side of this argument. The appellate courts found that defendants should not benefit just because the plaintiff had health insurance. If anyone should get the difference between what is billed and what is paid, it should be the injured party who bought the health insurance in the first place. Why should the big insurance companies benefit when it was the plaintiff who bought the health insurance? Why should the defendant who hurt someone get the benefit and not the injured party? Makes sense to me. Darn it!

Not only did it make sense, but it was also supported by the law. The plaintiff's bar was relying on the longstanding collateral source rule. This rule of law says that other sources of compensation an injured plaintiff may recover do not come into evidence and do not reduce the damages award. The biggest source of collateral compensation in most cases is insurance. This rule prevents the defense from telling a jury the plaintiff had insurance and her medical bills were paid by insurance, so the defense does not have to pay for her injuries. A jury never gets to know whether anyone had insurance. The collateral source rule had been around for a very long time and the appellate courts thought it was another good reason plaintiffs should get the windfall of billions of dollars.

COULD IT GET ANY WORSE?

Okay, so their arguments had won three out of four times, they made sense, and they were supported by the law. Anything else against us? Why yes, there was!

In 2011, shortly before oral argument in our *Howell* case, the California Supreme Court made history. For only the second time ever, a female was appointed as the chief justice. Tani Gorre Cantil-Sakauye was also the first Asian-Filipina American chief justice and she was brilliant. She was relatively young, well educated, highly respected, engaging, and did I mention brilliant? She was from a segment of lawyers who have been long underrepresented in our profession, and her appointment was rightly celebrated across the country. It was a very proud moment for all of us who practice law in California.

So what could be wrong with this? Well, just by chance, Chief Justice Canti-Sakauye had already ruled on our issue just before her new appointment. And you guessed it: she wrote one of the three appellate decisions against us!

Yes, the new chief justice had already analyzed all of our issues and in a very well-written opinion, decided we were dead wrong! She had plenty of reasons why the injured plaintiffs should receive the billions of dollars.

So not only was I going up against one of the strongest lobbyist groups in California, I now had a new chief justice who already had many well-thought-out reasons why I was completely wrong. I thought I was going down as a billion-dollar loser for sure!

YOU NEED A THEME

I was the first to speak that morning, and the last to speak. The seven justices all filed in and sat above me in their dark robes. A green light bulb turned on, literally. That was my cue, so I nervously stood and approached the enormous podium. *Why is everything so big in this courtroom?* I wondered. In my jury trials, some courtrooms do not even have podiums, let alone one I could put my whole suitcase on! Oh, that's right, everything is so big here because everything we were arguing was so big!

So what was I going to say? The law was against me, the facts were against me, and the brand-new chief justice wrote an opinion against me! I needed to come up with a theme! A theme is critical in any trial and will be explored further in the next chapter. But would a theme work with seven really smart justices when you only have a half hour, not weeks of trial? Yes, a good theme works with anyone! A good theme works with a politician (like it or hate it, think "Make America Great Again"), a company ("Just Do It," "The Happiest Place on Earth"), your personal life ("Happy wife, happy life!"), and many others.

So what was our theme? Like most good themes, it was short and simple. Here it is: there are no damages!

What is now called the "negotiated rate differential—" the difference between what a healthcare provider bills and what is accepted as payment— is simply not damages. Take our example above, the $80,000 difference between the $100,000 bill and the $20,000 the hospital took as payment from the health insurance provider. No one is owed the $80,000. The injured plaintiff is not out $80,000. The plaintiff does not owe $80,000 to anyone. The hospital is done. The hospital has accepted $20,000 as full payment and is not seeking any more money from anyone.

So what is the damage? What is the loss? What is the harm? Everyone is fully paid. The healthcare provider got all of the money it was seeking. The health insurer paid all of the money it had agreed to pay. The injured plaintiff did not pay any of that money. So where is the damage? This was our theme, no damage.

FINAL ARGUMENT

During my oral argument, there was some good news and some bad news. The bad news was I knew one of the seven justices was definitely going to rule against me. An appellate justice who was rotating onto the Supreme Court bench to fill a temporary vacancy seemed pretty upset with my argument.

The good news? Our theme was working! This temporarily sitting justice interrupted my argument and asked me why I had not mentioned the collateral source rule once. "I thought this case was about the collateral source rule; why are we not even talking about it?" she asked angrily. I, of course, calmly explained the collateral source rule applied to damages. So when analyzing the issue of the difference between what is billed versus what is paid, we must first address whether it was even damages. She didn't like my answer much. She definitely would not have liked my real reason!

My real reason for avoiding the collateral source rule was because it didn't help me! The real reason we were not arguing about the injured plaintiff having paid her insurance premiums or the big bad insurance companies getting over on the little guy is because it didn't help us! It was not our theme. While I did need to be able to explain all of these matters, I really needed to keep everyone on point. Our point. Our winning theme!

YOU WILL WIN, TOO!

The nerves went away pretty quickly, as is often the case when you are super prepared for any public speaking. There were no surprises in the oral argument, other than the fact there were no surprises. We were ready for every question and hypothetical thrown at us. Against all odds and one of the most influential lobbyist groups in America, we won! We won big. Six justices in our favor and only one against.

This is the case that put us on the map. Yes, beating the Consumer Attorneys of California for billions of dollars will get you noticed. Not only by the plaintiff's bar, for whom the verdict meant a loss of forty percent of more than $10 billion dollars every year, but by the media, the public, corporations, and of course, insurance companies. While they were all very appreciative at first, you are only as good as your last trial. And that is what I am after all, a trial attorney.

So while *Howell v. Hamilton Meats* may have been the biggest win of my career, it's really just a culmination of years of arguing damages at the trial level. This book will address ways that attorneys, insurance companies, corporations, and even individuals can obtain damage awards from juries that are fair, reasonable, and consistent with the law. You will learn how to defuse anger, accept responsibility, get defense verdicts even when you give a jury a defense number, advance your effective trial themes with every witness, and much more.

Some of this will be controversial. Some of it you will disagree with. But some of it you will need. You will need it to restore justice to our jury system. This book will help you even the playing field and obtain fair and reasonable compensation for all! Now sit back and enjoy the moment, dude!

CHAPTER 2

ACCEPT RESPONSIBILITY

ACCEPT RESPONSIBILITY IN EVERY CASE

In every jury trial, you must accept responsibility for something. Even if you're trying to obtain a defense verdict, you must accept responsibility. Not necessarily liability or negligence, but responsibility. In every single jury trial, no excuses.

Why? Because you must defuse the number one source of runaway jury verdicts: anger.

Remember, the defense must care about the plaintiff. In order to avoid a runaway jury verdict, the defense must care about what the plaintiff claims happened to her. At the very least, you must show the jury you care about the plaintiff. Accepting responsibility accomplishes this. If you care about the plaintiff, this will help defuse anger. This chapter will explain the reasons for this rule in detail and how you do it. I learned the importance of accepting responsibility a long time ago.

IF YOU CAN'T TAKE THE HEAT, GO TO GRANDMA'S HOUSE!

Growing up on Staten Island in New York, we lived for the summer. Sure, it was hot and muggy, and maybe there were days when you could barely breath outside, but at least we weren't in school. As kids, my younger sister and I would ride our bikes to our grandparents' house in the summers. We would head down our tree-lined street to the buzz of cicada bugs, humming loudly in all the towering green oak trees. That meant it was going to be a hot one!

We loved to go to my grandparents for two main reasons. First, they had candy. Second, they had air conditioning. Air conditioning was a big deal when I was growing up. We only had two in-the-window type air conditioners in my house. One was in my parents bedroom and the other was in the living/dining room. The one in the dining room was almost never turned on. At night, we had to beg to sleep on my parents' cool bedroom floor in our 1,100-square-foot ranch home. But when my parents got up in the morning to commute to their jobs in the city, the air conditioner was turned off. It was off until they got home at night. I'm not sure how, but they knew when they walked in at night if we had turned it on at all during the day. I sometimes wondered if my mom really did have eyes in the back of her head.

So off we would go to my grandparents in the late morning, when we just couldn't take the heat anymore. The short bike ride, on one-way side streets, was mostly downhill. We were supposed to stay together on our ride, but like most things in my life, it would sometimes become a competition to see who would get there first and "win." We would show up panting and sweating, dropping our bikes in their back yard. Up the steps we would race, into their old two-story brick home. Swing the back door open and there it was, the rush of coolness. *Aahh*, it felt like an ice chest. With big smiles on our sweaty faces, we would hug our grandmother and grandpa would yell, "Shut the door!"

We got the air conditioning, now bring on the candy! The air conditioner was blowing full blast, we had candy in our hands, a soda on the side table, my grandfather's recliner was fully back, and it was time to see which of the five TV channels were showing Abbott and Costello reruns. This was too good to be true! Well, unfortunately, it was.

After about an hour of doing absolutely nothing in wonderful cold air, my grandfather would start insisting we go outside. He would say, "Get out of the house. You can't just sit around and watch TV all day!" Oh, really? I would probably still be doing that if I wasn't pushed.

One day, my sister and I acquiesced and went outside into the unbearable heat. I played Little League at the time and my sister, Denise, played softball, so it was time for catch. We both had our gloves. We started throwing a rubber ball to each other. That was my grandfather's rule: No throwing a hard ball, or a baseball.

My grandparents' home had a small grass back yard, with one side abutting the back wall of a dry cleaner's. In this cinder-block wall, there were a couple of windows to allow that wonderful dry cleaner smell to escape.

My sister and I started with a rubber ball, but after a little while, that was no fun. So I got a baseball and began throwing some pretty impressive pitches. I remember throwing a perfect strike that my sister failed to catch. Denise's version is it was a wild pitch. Regardless, we broke the dry cleaner's window! And I was scared to death. I knew my grandfather was going to be very angry with me. But I walked into that air-conditioned house, which did not feel very good at that moment, and told my grandfather. He was livid!

My grandfather took me by the hand and said, "We are going to the dry cleaner's and you are going to take responsibility for this young man!" We walked around to the front of the building and into the dry cleaner's. My grandfather asked for the owner. When he came out, my grandfather said, "Tell him what you did." I was scared to death, but I somehow managed to eek out, "I broke your window, sir, with my baseball." The owner was surprised. He told us to hold on and he went to the back of the store. My grandfather was not happy.

When the owner returned a minute or two later—it seemed like an eternity—he had the ball in his hand. I still had no idea what to expect. The owner approached and handed me the ball. He said, "Son, I want to thank you for taking responsibility for your actions. Here is your baseball back." Yes! I had my ball back. The owner seemed pleased with me. I had done the right thing; I had taken responsibility. I guess it was time to go back to the air conditioning and candy!

As I turned and started to walk out of the store, with a big feeling of relief, I felt a pull on my collar, jerking me backwards. It was my grandfather. His hand was firmly on my shirt and neck, and he seemed even angrier than before. "Hold on," my grandfather said. "You are not done yet. You are going to pay this gentleman back for the window you broke."

My heart sank. I knew what that meant and it wasn't good. I knew I would be mowing lawns for the rest of the summer, just to pay the dry cleaner back for his window. Instead of being in the air conditioning watching TV, I was going to be cutting lawns in the sweltering heat.

EVERY CLOSING ARGUMENT

And, ladies and gentleman of the jury, I learned the meaning of the word "responsibility" that day. I learned "responsibility" is really two words: acceptance and accountability. I had accepted responsibility for the broken window, but I also had to be held accountable. I learned that lesson at twelve; it's time for the plaintiff to learn this lesson now. A defense verdict teaches the plaintiff this lesson and holds her accountable.

Yes, I tell this story of responsibility in just about every jury trial. Accepting responsibility for something must happen in every single jury trial. No exceptions.

This concept is not generally accepted by clients or defense lawyers. It's even somewhat controversial. Defense-minded folks are very skeptical of this approach. There are a lot of questions.

How can you accept responsibility and still get a defense verdict? Why would I accept responsibility when my client did not do anything wrong? Won't a jury be confused if we accept responsibility? It will not make sense and I will never get a defense verdict. And my client will never allow me to accept responsibility; he thinks he did nothing wrong even more than I do!

These are questions and concerns we hear in almost every jury trial. Many people disagree with this core concept for avoiding runaway jury verdicts. Most on the defense side of litigation have a very difficult time accepting responsibility when they did nothing wrong. Or when, maybe, they weren't perfect, but the plaintiff or someone else was mostly at fault.

Well, it's time to break the typical defense approach to jury trials. You must accept responsibility in every single jury trial.

THE POWER OF RESPONSIBILITY

Guess who else doesn't want you to accept responsibility? Plaintiff's counsel! I recently had a $7 million brain injury jury trial in Ventura, California, where the plaintiff's counsel refused to accept our stipulation to liability. Just before we began to pick a jury (which is a very good time to stipulate to liability), we stipulated to 100 percent liability on behalf of our employee driver and our corporate defendant. The judge asked the very experienced Los Angeles plaintiff's attorney if he accepted our stipulation of liability. Plaintiff's counsel said no. The judge said, let's proceed.

Wait, what? Why on earth would a plaintiff's lawyer ever choose to prove his case when the defense is willing to stipulate to it? The plaintiff has the burden of proof. So many things can go wrong in a jury trial, why risk it? Why would a plaintiff's lawyer ever not accept a stipulation to full liability? (I never knew you needed both sides to agree to a stipulation; I always thought any side could just stipulate to a material fact or liability. We ultimately had to file a new responsive pleading withdrawing our liability affirmative defenses to the complaint before the judge would finally exclude any further evidence on liability.)

The answer is simple: Plaintiff's attorneys want to prove liability so they can get the jury angry. They do not want the defense to accept responsibility. They do not want the defense to seem reasonable, to seem like we care. No, a good plaintiff's attorney wants to get the jury angry.

How do they do that? They tell the jury all of the mistakes the defendant made and all of the things the defense failed to do. They tell the jury how we don't care about the community, about the jurors friends and fellow citizens. How the defense's actions or inactions put everyone's loved ones at risk. In fact, when a good plaintiff's attorney is proving negligence, they are rarely focused on the incident. Rather, they're focused on the lack of training, or the failure to follow corporate rules, or to even have rules, or follow the law, or anything but the innocent mistake made by an employee.

WHY ACCEPT RESPONSIBILITY?

In just about every jury trial, everyone on the defense side fights to avoid accepting responsibility. Your client, the insurance company, your co-counsel, and even the plaintiff's counsel will fight you when you try to accept responsibility. But the last objection is most telling: The fact that plaintiff's counsel, who regularly achieves nuclear verdicts, doesn't want the defense to accept responsibility cannot be ignored. They will not accept your stipulation to partial or full liability for one reason: it works! Plaintiff's counsel knows that accepting responsibility will gut their chances of getting a runaway jury verdict. Accepting responsibility works!

Why does accepting responsibility work? There are three main reasons: it makes the defense team seem reasonable, it defuses anger, and it shifts the focus to other culpable parties.

1. APPEAR REASONABLE

First and foremost, taking responsibility makes anyone seem reasonable, not just a defendant. Generally, people are more inclined to listen to reasonable, agreeable people, as opposed to unreasonable people. Think about whom you'd rather talk to at a party: An affable, friendly person who takes responsibility for their life or someone who always blames everyone else? It is human nature to be attracted to the more reasonable person. And the most reasonable person in the room often wins!

It's therefore even more important to appear reasonable when you are trying to persuade someone. If you start an argument by telling the other person they are wrong, they will never listen to your points. Be agreeable, concede what you can, and win!

Benjamin Franklin knew this hundreds of years ago when he wrote in his autobiography:

> *When another asserted something that I thought an error, I denied myself the pleasure of contradicting him abruptly, and of showing him immediately some absurdity in his proposition. In answering I began by observing that in certain cases or circumstances his opinion would be right, but in the present case there appeared or seemed*

to me some difference, etc. I soon found the advantage of this change in my manner; the conversations I engaged in went on more pleasantly. The modest way in which I proposed my opinions procured them a readier reception and less contradiction. I had less mortification when I was found to be in the wrong, and I more easily prevailed with others to give up their mistakes and join with me when I happened to be in the right.

This is an important lesson in life, and it's even more important in court. Strive to be the most reasonable person in the room. Begin every argument by conceding something or appearing to be in agreement. It's a more pleasant approach for a judge or jury to listen to, and it's also more persuasive.

FORGET THE BATTLE, WIN THE WAR!

But defense lawyers want to fight everything. Literally fight every battle.

Not me. I want to win the war!

I will concede just about anything to win. I will say we are sorry, we were at fault, we are responsible—whatever it takes. You want to win? You want to avoid a runaway jury verdict? Then be the most reasonable person in the room and accept responsibility for something.

When a defense attorney denies all responsibility, the jury will instantly look for any hole in the defendant's argument. The jury will not be listening to what the defense lawyer is saying; they will be thinking about what else your client could have done to avoid this incident. Once there's a perceived flaw in a defendant's argument, the defendant's credibility begins to erode.

When contesting liability, accepting responsibility allows the defense to highlight how it acted as a reasonably prudent person or business under the circumstances. Similarly, it is just as important to accept responsibility when the defense is only partially liable. When partial liability is clear, accepting responsibility is the most reasonable position to present the jury. It allows the defense to defuse juror anger and focus the jury on the actions and fault of others. And win, of course!

2. DEFUSE JUROR ANGER

A second major advantage to accepting responsibility is it defuses juror anger. The goal of the best plaintiff's attorneys is simple: get the jury angry. Sympathy will get a plaintiff paid, but the real payday comes when a plaintiff's attorney can get a jury angry, especially at the defendant.

Anger is the number one motivator of runaway jury verdicts in America. For this reason, attorneys will constantly attempt to enrage and provoke extreme emotions from jurors.

So just as a good plaintiff's attorney looks for what will make a jury angry, the defense must figure out a way to defuse juror anger. Accepting responsibility is the best way to do this. Accepting some responsibility, even when requesting a defense verdict, allows you to take juror anger, which often arises through the plaintiff's attorney's use of reptile theory tactics, out of the equation. Moreover, acknowledging the defendant's fault or error— mea culpa—when accepting any portion of liability, similarly defuses juror anger. Employing these strategies early allows defense counsel to puncture a hole in the "anger balloon," preventing significant buildup that likely would result in the balloon "popping" later in the form of a runaway jury verdict.

3. SHIFT FOCUS TO OTHER'S COMPARATIVE FAULT

Another advantage to accepting responsibility is it allows you to blame everyone else. After accepting responsibility for your client's actions, you are able to shift the jury's focus to the other party's potential comparative fault. Accepting responsibility doesn't leave all other parties blameless. On the contrary, this strategy allows the jury to assess the culpability of other parties, including the plaintiff, who have failed to accept responsibility for anything. When the focus is shifted to the plaintiff's actions early in the trial, the jury will more closely scrutinize the plaintiff's arguments and identify more problems with the plaintiff's case and credibility.

Accepting responsibility is especially effective in shifting comparative fault when the defense also accepts some portion of liability. For example, the defense is able to argue to the jury, "You do not have to decide if we were negligent; what you have to decide is who else is negligent." In admitted liability cases, this technique arms the jury to assign substantial comparative fault to others who have failed to accept responsibility and appear unreasonable at trial.

HOW DO YOU ACCEPT RESPONSIBILITY?

There are three ways the defense may accept responsibility. It depends on what you're trying to accomplish. The first way is to accept responsibility for your client being totally at fault. The second is when your client is only partially at fault for the alleged wrongdoing. The final way is when you want a defense verdict and therefore are accepting responsibility, but not liability. As my law partner Cayce Lynch likes to say, accepting responsibility falls into three baskets, three designer baskets, of course. Let's discuss the first designer basket.

FIRST SCENARIO: 100 PERCENT LIABILITY

The first type of case, where you are completely at fault, no excuses, no one else to blame, is the easiest. Your client made a mistake, they hurt someone, were inattentive, or misunderstood something. Accept full responsibility, 100 percent. There is no one else to blame; it's all you.

Own it. Tell the jury you did it. We accept responsibility for our actions. Tell the jury to hold you and your client accountable. Yes, responsibility is really two words: acceptance and accountability. Hold us accountable.

Defense lawyers do not like this. It makes us uncomfortable. What if the jury really does hold us accountable? Uh oh, they may award the plaintiff money! Well, yes, of course they will. That's the whole reason we are here. The jury is here to award money, no other reason. Address it, own it.

Defense lawyers, in general, are loathe to address the most difficult parts of their case. They do not want to discuss it with the jury. They feel uneasy. They do not want the jury thinking about the problems with their case. Fight this urge! Accept full responsibility and tell the jury to hold you accountable. They are going to whether you tell them to or not. So own it!

Another basic but critical point in this regard: Never tell the jury you "stipulate to liability." Your client accepts responsibility. It's more powerful. The word "responsibility" means something to a jury. Do you teach your children to stipulate to negligence or accept responsibility for their actions? Which is more powerful: "We have entered into a stipulation of liability with the court?" Or, "We accept responsibility for our actions and we are here for you to hold us accountable?" Drop the legalese! Use words the jury understands and believes. Accept full responsibility when you are at fault and ask the jury to hold you accountable. It will be persuasive.

SECOND SCENARIO: PARTIAL LIABILITY

This is the scenario defendants and their lawyers struggle with the most. Why are we accepting any liability when it was really the plaintiff's fault? This accident would not have happened but for the plaintiff's own negligence, or stupidity. The plaintiff was drunk, the plaintiff was not watching where she was walking, the plaintiff violated company policy, the plaintiff caused her own comorbidity, the plaintiff was not an innocent investor, etc.

This belief in a plaintiff's culpability is often combined with the defense believing it had done nothing wrong or, at the very least, met the applicable standard of care. You hear such statements as, "Our product is safe if it is used as intended," or "We have been in business for over twenty years without a problem," or "We followed our employee handbook, which all of our employees were given," or "We can only make our property or equipment so safe," etc.

Does any of this sound familiar? Has anyone ever had a case where it's undisputed that fault lies mainly with the plaintiff? But no matter how many mock jury trials you have, the client always ends up with at least some small percentage of liability. No matter how many different arguments you make to show your client has no liability at all, there seems to always be a small percentage coming back to you and your client.

Well, if you're going to be attributed some small share of fault no matter what, then own it! If there is no escaping that your client will have 5 percent, 10 percent, or 20 percent of fault, why not accept liability? Why not stipulate to liability? Why not tell the jury you accept responsibility?

Why not? Ego! You think you can pull it off! The plaintiff has the burden of proof; you have to prove nothing. A lot can go wrong in a jury trial, so why help the plaintiff by stipulating to liability? Sure, you spent $50,000, $100,000, or more on mock jury simulations and expert jury consultants to give you the insight as to what a real jury may do. But that was a mock trial. You are no mock lawyer, you are a real trial lawyer.

And your client does not want you to stipulate to liability. They think the plaintiff was an idiot, or wrong, or a liar. You think so too. So does your spouse and friends when you tell them about the trial. You believe in your client. You want to prove to your client that you believe them, so you ask for a defense verdict. And the different mock jury scenarios all find your client only minimally at fault. So you have a chance. Maybe you can pull out a defense verdict against all odds?

Please fight this urge! This is how you get killed. Skilled plaintiff's counsel will kill you for not accepting any responsibility for your client's actions. Taking the typical defense approach of "deny, deny, deny" plays right into plaintiff's counsel's hands. This strategy of complete denial is consistently found in runaway jury verdicts. You need to change your approach! The "norm" for the defense industry is not working!

Remember what you are trying to do. You are trying to avoid a runaway jury verdict. You want to minimize damages. You are trying to defuse juror anger. You must seem like the most reasonable person in the room. The best way to do that? Accept responsibility for something! Accept responsibility when your sound research and common sense show that under just about every possible scenario, your client will have at least some small portion of liability.

HOW DO YOU ACCEPT RESPONSIBILITY WHEN ONLY PARTIALLY AT FAULT?

So how do you do it? How do you accept only partial liability? Start at the beginning and really own it! Tell the jury some version of the following in your opening statement:

> We accept responsibility in this case. My client was negligent. You will not have to decide if we were at fault. We were. You will not have to answer any juror questions on the special

verdict form at the end of this case as to whether we have responsibility in this case. We do. We accept liability for our actions. We are here for you to hold us accountable.

The plaintiff will present all types of arguments about things we have done wrong, things we could have done better, things we should have done more of. Listen to this evidence of course; listen to all of the evidence over the next few weeks. But remember, you will not have to decide whether any of this evidence is accurate or true. We were negligent. We made a mistake. You will not have to decide this. The thing you will have to decide is who else has fault for this accident.

And let's talk now about who else has responsibility for this accident. Well, despite counsel accepting no responsibility in her opening statement, the evidence will show the great majority of fault for these unfortunate events lies with the plaintiff herself. So what exactly did the plaintiff do in this case?

Do this in your opening statement and you will be well on your way to doing the number one thing to avoid a runaway jury verdict: showing you care. Accept responsibility for something the jury is going to find anyway and you will help defuse juror anger. If a jury is not angry at you or your client, the chances of a nuclear verdict are reduced greatly.

The one question you may receive from your clients is, "If you're going to accept liability on my behalf, tell me exactly what I did wrong. Tell me what you are going to tell that jury I did wrong." When the plaintiff was extremely careless or mostly at fault for an incident, your clients will naturally be resistant to accept any liability at all. It is also natural for the defense bar to want to please our clients. After all, unlike the plaintiff's bar, we hope to get repeat business from these same clients and hopefully a lot of business!

Fight this urge! You do not want to tell the jury what your client did wrong. You do not want to pick one or two things the plaintiff says your client failed to do and agree. Why do you not want to tell the jury exactly what your client did wrong?

The reason is fairly simple logic. What happens if the jury agrees with you but also believes your client was at fault for other reasons as well? For instance, if you tell the jury your client could have done X and ask the jury to hold him only 10 percent at fault, what happens if they also find he was at fault for Y and Z? Does his liability go up? Is your exposure greater now because you gave them something specific? Yes it is!

Let's say you listen to your client, who is concerned about you accepting fault. Your client insists you tell the jury exactly what he did wrong. So in your closing, you say the following:

> *Ladies and gentleman, you have heard a lot of evidence about the ten things we could have done, or could have done better, to avoid this accident. As you know, we disagree with many of these arguments. But we do agree with one of them. In hindsight, we could have had more security guards present. Because of this failure to have enough security personnel present, we believe we have minimal exposure in this case, no more than 10 percent liability.*

Sounds like a reasonable approach, right? Your client is happy. But what if the jury not only agrees with you that you should have had more security, but they also decide you should have done three other things? Your client should have had better lighting, more warning signs, and put up safety cones. So instead of just the one thing your client could have done better, he could have done a total of four things better. And because you told the jury one thing you did wrong equaled 10 percent liability, do four things wrong equal 40 percent fault for your client? I think it does! And in a purely comparative fault state like California, 40 percent of a big verdict like $20 million is a much bigger number than 10 percent. (The difference for the typical math-averse attorney would be $8 million versus $2 million owed by your client.)

This is a very real danger. Other than making a client who feels wrongly accused feel better, what does it really get you? Does it limit your risk any better than generally accepting fault? No. This is the better way to accept responsibility in your closing argument when your client has only partial liability:

> *We could have done more to avoid this unfortunate ac-*
> *cident. We wish we had done more, because no one ever*
> *wanted this tragedy to occur. We accept responsibility for*
> *our actions and we are here for you to hold us account-*
> *able. You will not have to decide whether we were neg-*
> *ligent. We were. We do have some fault for this accident.*
> *All you have to decide is how much liability we have and*
> *who else has responsibility. I respectfully suggest to you*
> *that when you prepare your special verdict form, you find*
> *my client had no more than 10 percent of the fault for this*
> *terrible accident. Who else has responsibility? Let's talk*
> *about the plaintiff's actions in this case....*

You have accepted responsibility. You have suggested a small percentage. Your percentage of fault is not tied to a specific negligent act that can then be added to or multiplied by the jury. The jury knows if they agree you were at fault, no matter what specifically they think your client did wrong, the reasonable amount of fault is only 10 percent.

Fight the urge to always appease your client. They will thank you after the verdict!

SCENARIO THREE: NO LIABILITY

The final scenario is no liability. Yes, you will accept responsibility even when you have no liability. You must accept responsibility in every single case, even if you have no liability. No exceptions. Remember, you must defuse juror anger to avoid a runaway jury verdict. Accepting responsibility is the best way to do this.

So how do you accept responsibility in a case where you have no liability? Isn't it going to sound like "lawyer speak," speaking out of both sides of your mouth? Hold us responsible, but give us a defense verdict?

Well, it actually sounds very reasonable to a jury. Here are some examples of things you may take responsibility for when you are telling the jury you have no liability:

- Accept responsibility for putting a safe product in the stream of commerce.
- Accept responsibility for maintaining a safe workplace.
- Accept responsibility for the defendant's response to alleged harassment in compliance with our own employee handbook.
- Accept responsibility for providing sound professional advice.
- Accept responsibility for meeting the applicable standard of care.

These examples provide the groundwork to defuse juror anger and highlight everything the defendant did right. For example, after accepting responsibility for putting a safe product in the stream of commerce, defense counsel should then highlight everything done to produce a safe product: thousands of hours of research and development, engineering, safety testing, drafting the instruction manual, independent certification, and training. In this specific example, defense counsel is not accepting any portion of liability, yet you are still accepting responsibility for something.

Accepting responsibility does not mean accepting full liability for the incident, or wrongful termination, or falling below the standard of care. In fact, as shown above, it does not require the defense to accept any liability at all. You need to evaluate every single case you are preparing for trial with an eye towards what you will accept responsibility for. The degree and manner of responsibility accepted depends on the individual case, but the strategy must be applied in every jury trial. A jury must understand that you do care about the plaintiff and this event. Accepting responsibility, not liability, will accomplish this.

And guess who will be accepting no responsibility at all? Correct: the plaintiff! That will not sit well with the jury. And you will be the most reasonable person in the room!

CONCLUSION

Yes, I tell the story of the broken window in just about every jury trial. You should, too! You need to find your own responsibility story. You have one. It may not involve your grandfather or a dry cleaner, but you have learned this lesson at some point in your life. You may have learned it on your own or maybe it was forced upon you, like it was for me. Find it, make it personal, and share it. The plaintiff's attorney will hate it. Perfect!

Be the most reasonable person in the room, in the courtroom. The jury will respond to you. They will connect with you.

They will like you. They will see that you care. They will not get angry. And, ultimately, the jury will resist the pleas of plaintiff's counsel for exorbitant damages and will return a verdict that is fair and just for all.

CHAPTER 3

ALWAYS GIVE A NUMBER

"IF THE EVIDENCE SUPPORTED it, would you have a problem with awarding a significant amount of money for plaintiff's harm, say $53 million?"

Until that point, the potential jurors had been sitting fairly stoically during this first day of jury selection. There were a lot of mundane questions and court procedures that had slowed folk's attention spans at best, and was probably sucking the life out of others. But this question about $53 million, by one of the top plaintiff attorneys in California, certainly got their attention. Some smiled, some shook their heads in disbelief, and others sat up and got ready to talk. And talk they did. They were "brutally honest," as plaintiff's counsel had asked them to be.

The discussion, artfully led by the plaintiff's attorney, ranged from whether anything was worth $53 million to jurors saying they'd need to see all of the evidence before making a decision. No one seemed to think it was *not* enough money, so I guess that was good.

WHAT TO DO?

So what do you do? You are the defense lawyer, potential ju-rors have just spent more than twenty minutes talking about whether they can keep an open mind about a brain injury case for a little girl being worth $53 million, and now it's your turn to talk with the jury. The judge had told you and plaintiff's counsel that he didn't want you arguing numbers to a jury in voir dire. But plaintiff's counsel insisted he had to know whether any potential jurors had some bias against awarding his client a just amount. But $53 million sure did sound like a pretty specific number to me. And it was. It was the num-ber that was repeated by plaintiff's counsel over the next two weeks, before the trial ultimately ended in a second mistrial.

So what do you do when you stand up in front of that potential jury for the first time? You could do what almost every defense lawyer in America would do: Nothing. That's right, nothing. Defense lawyers routinely shy away from the most difficult parts of their cases. Money, damages, is always a difficult part of any jury trial. It's tough to talk about in real life. It's difficult to talk to your parents about money, your kids, your friends, your co-workers. It can be even more difficult to discuss with a roomful of strangers who may decide your client's future.

And in this trial, the judge had told us not to argue dollar amounts. Defense lawyers are rule followers. We're pleasers. We want to be on the judge's good side. And this particular plain-tiff's counsel was definitely on the judge's bad side. He pushed the envelope with the judge by talking numbers and it was only the first day! If you do not discuss any numbers, the judge will be pleased with you. You will have followed the letter and spirit of the judge's ruling. You will have followed the rules, taken so-lace in that, slept well that evening, and even later told your defense buddies how outlandish plaintiff's counsel's actions were, flaunting the court's rules. How dare he!

But you will also be a loser. You will have gotten killed by a plaintiff's lawyer who has studied the psychology of jurors and knows he has set the bar at $53 million. The jury will think they are being empaneled to hear a $53 million case because you said nothing. And while you may have felt good about yourself and your moral compass, you will not have fulfilled your ethical duty to your client, to fight for justice. Again, justice does not just happen. It must be fought for; it must be earned.

FIGHT YOUR DEFENSIVE INSTINCTS

So what do you do? Do the opposite! Give the jurors a number! Fight the urge to be comfortable. Fight the inclination to just follow the defense herd. Fight for justice!

I did stand up and talk to the potential jurors. It would have been very easy for me to avoid this issue altogether. But that is not how you win. Shortly into my questioning, I said, "You heard plaintiff's counsel talk about millions of dollars. Well, that is a lot more money than I ever imagined he wanted. But let me ask you this: If the evidence supported a much lower damages award, let's say $500,000 or less, would you have a problem awarding only $500,000 or less? Might it be tough for some of you to tell a little girl, and her attorney, 'No, this case is not worth millions of dollars?' What do you think about this? How does it make you feel, that we injured this girl but we believe the evidence in this case will support an award of much less than the plaintiff's attorney is requesting, actually $500,000 or less? Does it just not sit well with anyone?"

And there it is. Our number is out there in front of the potential jurors three times. And that's not the end of it. We've started a discussion where our number is going to be a topic for fifteen or twenty minutes. The jurors now understand this is not a $53 million case. They know there is a dispute, and, in fact, it looks like it's going to be a fight. And of course there were no objections to this line of questioning from plaintiff's counsel, since he started it all.

ALWAYS GIVE A NUMBER!

This is probably the most controversial chapter in this book. Everyone pushes back when it comes to giving a damages number to a jury, especially if we want a defense verdict. *How on earth can you give the jury a number to award and still get a defense verdict? It makes no sense. You should not do it. You cannot ask the jury to award a defense damages amount and still get a defense verdict.*

A version of this refrain is heard in almost every jury trial I have. My response? Sorry, but you are dead wrong and I am doing it! Okay, my response varies depending on whether you are my client, the insurance company, co-counsel, one of my attorneys, or someone else. But my message, as controversial as it may be, is always the same: Yes, you definitely can ask the jury for a specific dollar amount and still get a defense verdict. I guarantee it.

Not only are the disbelievers often converts to this trial tactic, they are sometimes forever grateful. In fact, as I write this chapter, I just finished a $10 million brain injury trial in Southern California. Co-counsel and her separate client refused to give a number and were adamant that we not give the jury a number in opening and closing. We were all going for a defense verdict in this trial about a ball leaving the field of play at a sporting event, resulting in a brain injury to an innocent pedestrian. However, after weeks of trial and on day three of eight days of jury deliberations (yes, eight days), co-counsel thanked us for giving a number. It was obvious we were not getting a defense

ALWAYS GIVE A NUMBER

verdict from the jury's questions to the judge and co-counsel was clearly scared. Needless to say, it was not a defense verdict, but it was still a very big win for the defense. My co-counsel was very grateful I gave a number.

So the rule that you must give a defense number in every single jury trial is very simple:

You must give it early, and often, and it must never go up.

The how and why for this simple, but rarely followed, rule is explained in this chapter.

WHY GIVE A NUMBER?

What is the best way to get a large jury verdict? Ask for it!

No potential juror leaves for jury duty one day and tells her husband, "I'm off to jury duty, honey. We will probably award someone $50 million today."

No, the only way a jury comes up with these astronomical numbers is that some plaintiff's lawyer asked for it.

And who knows this is the best way to get a large jury verdict? That's right, plaintiff's attorneys.

The best plaintiff's lawyers in the country know asking for a large verdict starting at the beginning of trial can get them big results: $25 million, $50 million, or even over $100 million. It's almost unheard of for a jury to award a large, "runaway" verdict without hearing a proposed dollar amount from plaintiff's counsel. Most jurors never walk into a courtroom thinking anything is worth $20 million or more. But after plaintiff's counsel starts talking about a huge number in voir dire, and then for the next few weeks through closing arguments, it doesn't seem so outrageous.

In many instances, the jury doesn't award the huge number plaintiff's counsel requested. They will often give a much lower number, even less than half of what was requested. And juries will think the defense attorney is happy with the verdict. Happy because the defense did not give any number, but the award is less than half of what plaintiff's counsel requested. But half of $25 million, $50 million, or $100 million is still huge. It will probably be the biggest loss of any defense counsel's career. Don't let it be your biggest loss!

WHEN DO YOU GIVE A NUMBER?

A number must be given early in a trial. Ideally during voir dire, but no later than your opening statement. Who knows this to be true? You guessed it: plaintiff's counsel. Good plaintiff's counsel will tell a jury their number as early as they can. Why? It's called priming.

Plaintiff's counsel will "prime" the jury by starting early and repeating a large number they are asking the jury to award. The psychology of "priming" is explained as follows:

> Priming is a technique used to influence (i.e., control) attention and memory, and it can have significant impacts on decision-making. Specifically, priming is an implicit memory effect in which exposure to a stimulus influences a response to a later stimulus. This means that later experiences of the stimulus will be processed more quickly by the brain.

Kanasky, Bill, Jr., Ph.D. (April 2014). Debunking and Redefining the Plaintiff Reptile Theory. *For the Defense*, 18.

In the context of determining a damages award, a jury that has been primed by repeatedly hearing the plaintiff's requested damages number will be more likely to arrive at a number close to the plaintiff's number. Although it's psychology, it's by no means rocket science.

For instance, if a juror is asked on day one of a trial how he feels about awarding $35 million if the evidence supports it, and on day two he is told by plaintiff's counsel the evidence will show this is a $35 million case, and then the number $35 million is worked into most days of the trial, and, finally, the juror is told a month later in plaintiff's counsel's closing argument that the evidence *did* show this was a $35 million case—what do you think the jury is going to do with this repeated information? Especially if defense counsel, in closing argument, says this case is not worth $35 million and maybe gives jurors a much smaller number for the first time a month later?

Until defense counsel, in closing argument, told the jury they must be fair and reasonable, the jurors thought they were deciding whether the case was worth $35 million. Now, to hear at the end of the trial they must be fair and reasonable or even award a much lower number, the jury is going to throw it out. They are going to wonder what trial the defense attorney has been sitting through. The jury will have been primed for a month that this is a $35 million case. They may not award that full amount, but I guarantee half of $35 million is way, way more than what the defense attorney told his *former* client this case was worth!

NO EXCUSES!

Very often I'm told by defense counsel, "I cannot give a number early because I do not know my number yet. I have to hear all of the evidence first, especially some of the expert opinions. I will be able to give a number in closing."

Wrong. Figure it out and figure it out now. You do not have to give an exact number. I never give an exact number until closing argument. Tell the jury early the evidence will show this case is worth X or less. For instance, "We believe the evidence will show the plaintiff is entitled to an award of $500,000 or less." Your ultimate number in closing may be $500,000, it may be $413,795.23, or it may be less.

Remember, the concept of priming is not a plaintiff-only concept. There is no such thing as a plaintiff's attorney psychology degree. Psychology is the study of the human mind and behavior, not the study of the plaintiff's attorney's mind and behavior! What works for plaintiff attorneys works for defense attorneys. You must use the same psychology the plaintiff's bar is using. No excuses.

GIVE IT OFTEN

The primacy and recency effect is the concept that people tend to remember information presented in the beginning (primacy) and the end (recency) of a learning episode. This is true in a jury trial. You must at least give the jury your defense number in the beginning and the end of every jury trial.

But what about everything between voir dire and closing? It could be weeks, even months. The good plaintiff's attorneys work their numbers into their presentation of the evidence as often as they can. They are getting their number in front of the jury by asking questions of their witnesses that either include their number, or elicit their number. If some is good, more is better.

Again, the same is true for the defense. You must get your number in front of the jury after opening and before closing. You should get your number into evidence during the plaintiff's case. You cannot wait until it's your turn to present evidence to reintroduce your number. Too much time will have passed. The jury must hear your number during the plaintiff's case.

GIVE YOUR ECONOMIC NUMBER

So, how do you get the defense's damage number in front of the jury when plaintiff's counsel is putting on her case? Let's start first with economic damages. A great way to work in the defense's economic numbers is through plaintiff's experts. Specifically, ask the plaintiff's doctors if they are aware the defense has an expert who has a plan to get the plaintiff better and it costs much less than the plaintiff's plan? For instance, "Dr. Jones, are you aware Dr. Smith has a plan to provide the plaintiff with better care and it only costs $100,000, not the $2.5 million you are claiming? You are familiar with Dr. Smith, right? You have read his deposition transcript? You understand it is Dr. Smith's opinion that if the plaintiff spends $100,000, she will be well on the road to recovery? I know, you don't think $100,000 is enough, right? But you will agree with me, doctor, that $100,000 is a significant sum of money, right? I know you don't think it's enough in this instance, but I'm sure you will agree, taken on its own, $100,000 is a significant sum of money?"

In this cross-examination, the defense attorney got his economic number in front of the jury five times. That's five times more than just about any defense lawyer in America. It doesn't matter how the doctor answers these questions. Who knows, you may even get a little gem with his answers, especially if a doctor tells a jury $100,000 is not significant.

Don't stop there. Try getting your economic damages number in with other plaintiff witnesses as well. "Dr. Treater, you don't have a plan to get the plaintiff better now; you just treated her, right? Dr. Treater, are you aware our expert, Dr. Jones, has a plan to get the plaintiff better and it costs about $100,000? Given this is not your expertise, would you defer to Dr. Jones and his $100,000 plan?"

Or maybe try, "Doctor I told the jury in my opening that the evidence would support a verdict of $500,000 or less, did you know that?" (Objection, maybe? Keep going!) "Your life-care plan alone is greater than what I told the jury I thought this whole case was worth. Doctor, is the cost of your plan alone more than $500,000? Doctor, does your plan, which exceeds my $500,000 total estimate, at least include compensation for the plaintiff's pain and suffering?"

Many of these questions may be objected to. Maybe not. Some objections may be sustained, maybe not. But add up the number of times you mentioned your defense number. If the jury could hear your number this many times, you are winning.

GIVE YOUR NON-ECONOMIC NUMBER

Getting your pain and suffering number in front of the jury during the plaintiff's case in chief is much more difficult. You have to be creative to bring out evidence to support your non-economic damages number through plaintiff's witnesses. It can be done, but you must be very careful.

One way to do it is through the plaintiff or the plaintiff's family and friends. Here's an example of how to get your emotional distress or pain and suffering number in front of a jury during the plaintiff's case.

I recently tried a $12 million product liability case in federal court. We were not only up against the best plaintiff's lawyer in San Diego, it was truly a tragic case. The plaintiff was a seven-year-old boy who lit his polo shirt on fire while playing with a cigarette lighter with his younger brother. The two had snuck away into their neighbor's yard with the lighter. The plaintiff held a small flower while his younger brother lit it. When it got too hot, the young plaintiff dropped it onto his button-down polo shirt and it immediately caught fire. The panicked boy began to flap his shirt to put out the fire, but it only caused the fire to grow bigger. He then ran around the yard, essentially on fire, until his dad came out to save him.

The young boy had severe third-degree burns on most of his body. He was hospitalized for two months and his mother stayed by his bedside every night. The trial took place 13 years later, when the boy, now a young man, was twenty years old. Unfortunately, his injuries had not healed with the passage of time. Despite some plastic surgeries, the scarring across his torso was terrible. The jury was not only able to see photos of the horrific burns and operations from when he was a boy, they could see the lifelong scars now. This young man would never take off his shirt, even to go to the beach or swimming, or when he was intimate with his girlfriend. These injuries were real and heart-wrenching, and all there for the jury to see.

Now, you may be thinking that if you play with fire, you will get burned. Good, that means you're on the defense side of this battle! But this was truly a tragic case. The injuries to this child were painful, disfiguring, and permanent. It was clear the jury felt very strongly for this boy and his family.

The plaintiff also had experts who were very critical of the shirt that was manufactured by my client in China. According to those experts, our shirts were not 100 percent cotton as our labels represented. Instead, our shirts contained a deadly blend of rayon and nylon, which, when combined with cotton, acted as an ignition source, causing the shirt to burn quicker and hotter than if it was all cotton. It was like a torch. Even worse, the rayon and nylon particles caused the shirt to melt against the boy's upper body, causing more severe burns than an all-cotton shirt would have caused.

We wanted a defense verdict. But we gave the jury a number early and often. Our number, first shared with the jury in voir dire, was $500,000 or less. The plaintiff's number was $12 million. Most of the damages in this case were non-economic. The scars were never going to get any better. The photos of the burns at the time of the accident and while he was in the hospital were terrible. Unfortunately, there was not much doctors could do now for this young man. This trial was about the pain and suffering, disfigurement, loss of enjoyment of life, emotional distress, humiliation, etc., that this young man suffered for the last decade and will continue to suffer for the rest of his life.

BE NICE!

So how do you get your pain and suffering number in front of a jury during the plaintiff's case in chief? How do you use plaintiff's witnesses to get your number into evidence instead of waiting weeks until it's your time to present a defense? Well, you must be creative, careful, and very nice!

In this trial, I took a chance with the brother. Remember, ten years earlier the brother had been playing with fire and was involved in this accident. He was a very nice young man on the stand. He deserved to be treated respectfully as we went over the facts of the accident. He was soft-spoken, but direct and honest. So at the very end of my cross-exam, I decided to take a chance and ended with this:

"Sir, would $500,000 have a significant impact on you and your family?"

At this point, there could have possibly been an objection. If there were, the jury would still have heard our number during the plaintiff's case. The jury would remember they were not in a trial that was only about whether the plaintiff's injuries were worth $12 million. They were hearing evidence of whether this case was worth $500,000 or less.

Hearing no objections, the young man responded, "Are you serious?"

Uh-oh. What had I done? My team never asked this question in deposition, and I did not expect them to, so I had no idea what his response would be. During that brief pause, I, for a second, was pretty worried. But then the brother went on:

"Sir, my family and I live in a trailer home near the Mexico border. We do not have much, sir. So, yes, $500,000 is significant; $500,000 would change our lives."

I had no further questions. His answers were honest and real, just like the testimony I had heard from him earlier. I took a chance with a relative of the plaintiff. Maybe someone who had not been coached as much as a plaintiff would be. Someone who had not been sitting through the trial and probably had no idea his brother's attorneys were asking for $12 million. His answer was extremely helpful for advancing our number to the jury early and often.

So what did the jury do? Read the coming section below on defense verdicts.

IT NEVER GOES UP

The number you give the jury at the beginning of trial can never go up. I thought this was common sense, but we learned the hard way it apparently isn't.

We were parachuted in shortly before trial to act as monitoring counsel for another defense firm in a very large brain injury case against the most infamous plaintiff's lawyer in California. This lawyer has written a book and is well-known for his unconventional antics to appeal to a jury's emotions. He has even worn a chicken suit during closing argument. Yes, a full-on costume of a mascot chicken, during closing argument. And the worst part is, he is really good.

As this was an admitted liability accident, it was a damages-only case. Giving the jury a number and really owning it is especially critical when the only real issue in a trial is damages. At this point in my career, I knew we had to get the lead defense counsel to give a number early and often. Not surprisingly, it was a battle. The defense counsel wasn't sure of his exact number. He had never given a number during voir dire. How do you do it? Why would you do it?

After much effort, my partner was able to persuade lead counsel to come up with a number and ask the jury about that number in voir dire. He asked the jury only one question about our number. Hearing no response, he moved on. My partner was unable to persuade counsel to give our number during opening statements or at any other point before closing arguments. Of course the extremely skilled plaintiff's attorney was working in his numbers every chance he got over the next month of the trial.

So how could this trial have gone any worse for the defense? I received a call from my partner before closing arguments. She told me defense counsel wanted to double his number for the jury! Yes, defense counsel had briefly mentioned $1.2 million during voir dire and now, in closing, he wanted to request an award of about $2.4 million.

What? We let him pick the number to tell the jury a month earlier and now he wanted to double it? No way—you can't do that. Plaintiff's counsel will crucify you in rebuttal. You will lose credibility in front of the jury. They will think you heard something during the past month that caused you to lose confidence in your own case. Why should they go with either defense number? It keeps changing.

So what happened? Defense counsel doubled his number and the plaintiff's counsel killed him in rebuttal. It was brutal. What did the jury do? They awarded $24 million for an alleged mild traumatic brain injury in Los Angeles.

What did we learn? A lesson I think we all already knew: Your number can never go up! The reasons are obvious. The results can be drastic. And that, ladies and gentlemen, is why we added to the rule: Always give a number, give it early and often, and *it never goes up*!

GIVE A NUMBER AND GET A DEFENSE VERDICT

You must give the jury a number in every single trial, even when you are seeking a defense verdict. Yes, it's possible to get a defense verdict *even if you give a number to the jury*. In the terrible child burn victim trial, we asked for a defense verdict for our polo shirt manufacturer but also gave the number $500,000 or less. Over the course of three weeks and listening to all of the evidence, the jury was not confused. They understood we wanted a defense verdict the whole time, even though we had given them a number. Fortunately, we received a defense verdict—not $500,000 or less, but also not the $12 million plaintiff's counsel had asked for. You can give the jury a defense number and still get a defense verdict. We literally do it all the time.

A large majority of the defense bar and insurance professionals believe it's a sign of weakness to offer a verdict amount to a jury when you really want a defense verdict. You are speaking out of both sides of your mouth. How is a jury going to believe you when you don't even believe yourself? In one instance, these folks are correct.

Let's say in a three-week jury trial the defense argues for no liability the whole time. If the first time the jury hears a number is in closing, then we agree, it's a sign of weakness. The defense has heard something in the last three weeks that has concerned it enough to give the jury a number for the first time.

Remember, the rule is you must give a number early and often. You cannot give your number for the first time in closing argument and expect a jury to take you or your number seriously. If you give a number at the beginning of trial, while asking for a defense verdict, and explain why you are presenting the jury with a proposed dollar amount, it will make sense to the jury and will not be a sign of weakness. In fact, a 2016 University of Iowa law review article found the exact opposite. This research showed you are more likely to get a defense verdict when you give the jury a defense number. Yes, give the jury a number and you are more likely to get a defense verdict. Don't believe me, believe the science!

WHAT DO YOU SAY WHEN SEEKING A DEFENSE VERDICT?

Here are some ways you can get your number in front of a jury early, during voir dire, even when asking for a defense verdict:

- Tell potential jurors you will be asking for a defense verdict or to award much less money than the plaintiff is asking for.

- Ask the jurors, "If the evidence shows, in your opinion, our client was not responsible for the plaintiff's fall, would you be able to give little or no money to the plaintiff and award a defense verdict?"

- "If the plaintiff is asking for more than $10 million in damages, but you believe the evidence supports an award of, say, $500,000 or less, would you be able to put aside sympathy for the plaintiff and award $500,000 or less?"

- "Same question, ladies and gentleman, but for a defense verdict. You heard the judge read off a list of experts who are going to testify in this case. If you find some of them to be persuasive and if the evidence supports it, are you going to be comfortable saying no to the plaintiff's request for millions of dollars and return a defense verdict?"

- "Does anyone believe just because there was an accident on our client's premises/vehicle/advice, etc., that we should pay the plaintiff whatever she asks for?"

Those are just a few examples. Stay on topic. Ask the jury how it makes them "feel." Do they understand why you are mentioning a number if you believe the evidence supports a defense verdict? You have an obligation to address all of the issues that will be presented to jurors over the course of the trial and explain that they will hear a lot of evidence about damages. Ask them how it makes them feel that you're mentioning a damages number even though you believe the evidence will support a defense verdict?

It can be done. You can get a defense verdict even when you give the jury a damages number. They will know what you want. Explain it, talk to them. A jury gets it. You will get many, many defense verdicts even with giving a number. Most important, if your number is reasonable and fair, and mentioned early and often, you will never be the victim of a runaway jury verdict.

CHAPTER 4

PAIN AND SUFFERING

IT WAS AS GOOD as I had feared it would be. And by good, I mean scary good. Plaintiff's counsel had just finished his closing argument in an admitted liability and stipulated economic damages case. He was the first president ever of the world-famous Gerry Spence Trial Academy not named Gerry Spence. He was by far the best lawyer I had tried a case against at that point in my career, and he had gone at me pretty hard with the jury. We had stipulated to liability, causation, and all economic damages. We had no experts, no witnesses, and absolutely no evidence. When the judge asked us to present our case, I stood up and told the jury we rested. To say I was a little worried would be an understatement.

Plaintiff's counsel had asked the jury to award over $3 million, and he made some very compelling arguments. He was trying to get the jury angry and it may have been working. He referred to our corporate client as driving a "meat truck." He asked the jury to imagine driving through an intersection in San Diego when suddenly a meat truck slams right into you, changing your life forever, taking away your life's passion, competitive surfing. How much would you want to be paid to have been in that car that day? How much would you want to be paid to not be able to pursue your passion?

He also asked the jury to award $100,000 a screw. Yes, $100,000 for every screw used in the plaintiff's neck for her two neck-fusion surgeries. He talked about the years, months, weeks, days, minutes, and seconds of pain the plaintiff had been forced to endure and put a dollar amount on each of these, totaling millions of dollars.

But it didn't end there. He also went at us, my associate and me. He told a story of growing up in a small, working class town where he worked as a boy in his father's bar. One day, two men in dark suits came into the bar. They were with the government. They told his father that he could not work in that bar because he was too young. Plaintiff's counsel told himself that day as a little boy that he would never let the men in the dark suits tell him what to do. And now it was time for you, the jury, to tell these two defense lawyers in their dark suits the same thing! He went on to say that if the jury awarded the plaintiff our much lower numbers, we would be outside high-fiving each other as we drove away in my black Mercedes. (I did not object, but it was actually a dark blue Mercedes.)

So what do you do? Most people would say this is the type of case you settle. But plaintiff's counsel would not take the million-dollar policy and claimed the insurance policy limits were blown wide open. You have no evidence. You have stipulated to literally everything except for the amount of pain and suffering. So, really, what do you do?

Well, you do something defense lawyers across America almost never do: you argue pain and suffering! And you better be good at it, because you have nothing else! You have no experts, no witnesses, no evidence of any kind. All you have is argument—argument about the only thing in dispute, non-economic damages.

NOTHING MORE IMPORTANT THAN PAIN AND SUFFERING

This is the most important chapter in the book. Simply put, these words have never been written before. This is the chapter my partners did not want me to write. This advice is what separates a good defense lawyer from a great defense lawyer. This is where I give away the playbook. All of my "secrets" will be out in the open, for both plaintiff and defense attorneys to see.

There are many books, articles, seminars, conferences, camps, and other training for plaintiff's lawyers to learn how to argue non-economic damages, or pain and suffering. If you are a plaintiff's lawyer, this is your bread and butter. This is how you get paid. The more damages you can convince a jury to award, the more money goes in your pocket. We defense lawyers? Not so much. We get paid by the hour, win or lose. We do not receive 40 percent of any verdict or settlement, or a portion of any savings we achieve for our clients. Consequently, defense lawyers must find their motivation to win from somewhere other than money.

So how do most defense lawyers argue non-economic damages to avoid runaway jury verdicts? They don't! They literally make no arguments about non-economic damages at all.

Non-economic damages are generally the biggest component of any runaway jury verdict. Think about it, does anyone ever scratch their head in wonderment when a jury awards all of the medical treatment a severely injured plaintiff needs to recover and live their lives? Does anyone question why someone who was wrongfully terminated from her job is awarded all of her lost earnings? No, of course not. We all agree an injured person should get the medical care they need and should be compensated for their lost wages. The shocking jury verdicts are when a plantiff is awarded a relatively small amount of economic damages, but then an astronomical amount in pain and suffering.

For example, $1 million for all of the plaintiff's past and future medical care and then $10 million or more in pain and suffering: that is a runaway jury verdict.

WE ARE RULE FOLLOWERS!

Research shows that in the large majority of these trials, defense counsel didn't argue non-economic damages at all. Seems unimaginable, right? Such a large component of a potential adverse jury verdict, and most defense lawyers don't even address it in closing argument. In one recent trial, defense counsel said, "As to non-economic damages, I have no opinion on that. I leave non-economic damages to you." What? No opinion as to the largest component of a runaway jury verdict? No opinion as to what the plaintiff's attorney believes is worth over $40 million in that trial? You can imagine what happened. It was disastrous.

But these same defense lawyers who will not touch non-economic damages will argue the heck out of economic damages. In fact, most defense lawyers love to argue economic damages. We love to learn the science and find flaws in our opponent's scientific evidence and experts. Defense lawyers find comfort in science. There are rules in science and predictable outcomes. Defense lawyers are rule followers!

These defense lawyers will spend quite a bit of time explaining how the defense experts are right and the plaintiff's experts are all wrong. They will go into excruciating details about the science, about the data, about reading x-rays and charts, medical journals and studies, and differential diagnoses, and the anatomy, and anything else these "frustrated doctors" are comfortable arguing. But these same defense lawyers will not spend any time on the biggest part of any nuclear verdict, pain and suffering!

HOW DO DEFENSE LAWYERS ARGUE PAIN AND SUFFERING?

And what about the small minority of defense attorneys who do argue non-economic damages? What approach do they use? Typically, these defense lawyers simply recite the law on damages and tell the jury they must be fair and reasonable. They may say the plaintiff's attorney's number is unreasonable. You must be fair and reasonable, like it says in the jury instructions.

That is not an argument! Telling a story about bad people kicking you out of your dad's bar as a child, that is an argument. The defense attorney's response to that and similar plaintiff's attorneys' stories, accompanied by a request for tens of millions of dollars, is most often that the jury must follow the law. They remind the jury that the award must be fair and reasonable. And we all know that $20 million or $30 million is not fair. It is not just. They'll tell the jury, "I know when you go back and deliberate, you will reach a fair and reasonable amount to compensate the plaintiff's pain and suffering, and it will not be tens of millions of dollars."

Again, nice try, at least. Better than not addressing non-economic damages at all. But it is not persuasive. It is not compelling. Reciting the law is not a real argument. It is not a story that connects the defense lawyer or his client with the jury. It does not resonate with the jury's value system or hit them on an emotional level. You need to really argue damages.

So how do you stand up in front of a jury in closing argument and argue damages?

HOW TO ARGUE NON-ECONOMIC DAMAGES

There are two ways, I believe, you should look at non-economic damages, or pain and suffering. They are:

1. What is the impact of this accident on the plaintiff's life, and
2. What is the impact of money on the plaintiff's life?

3. This is what we say to the jury in every single jury trial. What is the plaintiff's life really like after the incident and what is the value of money to the plaintiff?

First, you must talk to the jury about how the accident has impacted the plaintiff. Is the plaintiff's life really as bad as portrayed by counsel? Tell the other side of the story.

Second—and this is the crux of arguing non-economic damages—talk about the impact of money on the plaintiff's life. How will the money you are asking the jury to award have a real and meaningful impact on the plaintiff's life? This concept may be the most important one in the book. Most defense lawyers shy away from talking about money or other difficult issues. The impact of money on the plaintiff's life must be addressed head-on. You must use real-life examples of what the plaintiff can do with the money you are recommending and how this addresses the different elements of non-economic damages, such as anxiety, emotional distress, etc. This chapter will discuss in detail how you come up with these examples through discovery and creativity.

IMPACT OF THE ACCIDENT

The first prong of arguing non-economic damages should be the easy part for most defense lawyers. We are skeptical by nature. We are used to having to work to find the truth, find out what is really going on with the plaintiff. Who is telling the truth? Who is possibly exaggerating their claims? Defense lawyers can do this. There are two sides to every story and it is your job to tell it.

How? First, defense counsel must paint a picture for the jury detailing what the plaintiff's life is really like now and what it may realistically look like in the future. In every case, look at what the plaintiff could do before the accident versus what she's unable to do after the accident. Or the plaintiff's life before and after she was terminated from her job, or before and after she received our alleged negligent advice, or whatever the wrongdoing may have been. The defense must find a way to paint a positive picture of the plaintiff's life. Defense counsel must analyze the plaintiff's post-accident life and tie in any defense number for pain and suffering.

Let's look at the *Howell* case, for example. The plaintiff claimed her life had been changed forever. She could not pursue her passion. Surfing defined her. She had always been athletic, but surfing and excelling at surfing had really been her calling. Now Ms. Howell could no longer surf semi-professionally. She could not surf as big of waves as she used to, she did not get as much enjoyment out of surfing because of her limitations, she could not run as far, and she was not as active as she used to be before the accident. She was no longer the same vibrant, energetic woman she used to be before our meat truck tragically changed her life forever, allegedly.

That was one side of the story. What about the other side? Well, both the plaintiff and her husband testified that after the accident and multiple neck-fusion surgeries, she could do just about everything she enjoyed doing before the accident. She did these activities somewhat less frequently and in a more restricted manner, but she could still surf, run, and hike. She did yoga, volunteered for charities, and was active with her husband. The plaintiff's doctors agreed her surgeries were a success and with hard work, she could continue to improve. There were some very positive things in her life and it was our job to let the jury know about them.

In closing argument, I walked the jury through a typical day in the plaintiff's life—she woke up at 6:30 a.m., walked her dogs, checked the internet for news, cooked breakfast for her husband, gardened with her dogs, checked the internet for surf conditions, went surfing if the conditions were good, completed household chores, read, made dinner for her husband, and spent time with her husband in the evening doing crossword puzzles and watching TV. Not a terrible life, right? While the accident certainly impacted her life, by the time of the trial, things had improved greatly. Her life was not as bad as the picture the plaintiff's attorney originally painted for the jury.

A positive perspective on the plaintiff's life after the accident supports a much lower number for pain and suffering. Tell the good news story. Tell the truth and argue for a number that is more fair and reasonably tied to the plaintiff's current lifestyle.

IMPACT OF MONEY

The second element to arguing pain and suffering is the most important: What is the impact of money on the plaintiff's life? What is the value of money to the plaintiff?

Defendants commonly hear plaintiff's attorneys say that they "take the plaintiff as we find them" when arguing the defense is responsible for injuries sustained by an "unusually susceptible plaintiff" (CACI 3928). While this is true with respect to medical damages, it's also true when it comes to jury awards for pain and suffering. Any dollar amount the jury awards must be fair and reasonable to *this plaintiff* based on the impact the money will have on the plaintiff's life. We take the plaintiff as we find him, so let's look at how we find him.

1. PLAINTIFF'S PASSIONS

When evaluating and arguing the impact of money on a plaintiff's life, defense counsel must relate the value of money to activities or hobbies the plaintiff enjoys. What is the plaintiff's passion in life? What did the plaintiff like to do for fun before this

57

accident? Who *was* this plaintiff? Ask the plaintiff these questions in her deposition. Any pain and suffering award should try to give the plaintiff back some of the enjoyment in her life she claims she lost.

And don't worry if you failed to ask the plaintiff in her deposition what her passion is. You can rest assured that during the trial every good plaintiff's attorney will let the jury know what his client's passion was before the accident. All good plaintiff's lawyers will make their case about their client's inability to follow their dreams or live their passion. The trial will be about the loss of the true essence of who that plaintiff was before this terrible incident. That loss of true self is much, much greater than any economic loss. Unless you want to get killed with a nuclear non-economic damages verdict, you better find out who that plaintiff truly is.

In the *Howell* closing argument, I explained that $100,000 equates to many surfboards, lots of surf wax, or gas money to surf North San Diego County beaches. It's a lot of surfing trips to exotic beaches. It's a large amount of gardening supplies, books, and yoga classes. One hundred thousand dollars would provide countless runs with her dogs, hikes, and dinners with her husband. It was real money to this plaintiff. It would have a real impact on her life and she deserved that. We hurt her and she deserved to have some peace and joy in her life. One hundred thousand dollars would do this.

2. HAPPY CAMPERS?

What is the number one thing plaintiffs say they liked to do for fun before an accident? How did they like to spend their free time? What gave them joy? The answer is camping.

Yes, we see camping and hiking come up all the time as things the plaintiff liked to do before the accident. Why? Of all the possible hobbies and activities out there, why would a plaintiff tell the jury camping or hiking?

First, camping and hiking are simple, down-to-earth activities. A plaintiff does not want to come across as well-to-do or better than the jury. They want to be seen as simple folk who enjoy doing simple things with family and friends that cost very little money. They want to relate to the jury and have jurors think they are not in this for the money.

Second, camping is somewhat physical. If you are severely or catastrophically injured, you cannot camp anymore. That simple pleasure has been taken away from you. You can no longer physically get into the mountains, or hike to your campsite, or carry your tent and equipment. You cannot enjoy the things you used to and a jury will clearly understand why.

So what do you do with this? How can you justify a number to the jury that will not allow the plaintiff to find joy in her life? No matter how much money you suggest, a severely injured plaintiff will never be able to climb a trail again or put up a tent or show her son how to start a fire in the woods. Our client has taken this simple pleasure away from the plaintiff forever. She will never be made whole.

Wrong! Figure out how to get the plaintiff this pleasure, this joy, back in her life. Examine what the plaintiff has lost. What has she really lost by not being able to camp because of this accident? At the core of it, what does she miss about it today? What is it about camping or hiking or many other activities a plaintiff will mention that she truly misses?

The answer is shared experiences. Sharing experiences with family and friends. Being around the fire telling stories with your brother or your son or your dad or your best friend. Sharing laughter, joy, wonderment, beauty, pain, silence, nature, companionship, boredom, and everything else with a loved one. It's rare a plaintiff will testify they liked doing something alone and sharing it with no one. We are social creatures by design. That is the essence of a plaintiff's loss. No matter what they tell you the activity was, at the heart of it, what is missing is a shared experience with loved ones.

So how do you give this back to a plaintiff? How do you help make a plaintiff whole if the jury awards your non-economic damages number? What will the plaintiff be able to do with your dollar amount to get back some of that joy and lost common experience? What exactly will your money do for the plaintiff if she can't pursue her passion?

Get to know your plaintiff. Where does she live, where did she used to vacation, where are her family and friends now? Who are her family and friends? What did they like to do for fun with the plaintiff? If she can no longer camp, what kind of shared experiences can she do? How can she spend time with family and friends? If she can't travel to her loved ones, bring her loved ones to her. Your number could pay for family gatherings, for instance. If the plaintiff can't get on a plane to go camping in Yellowstone National Park with family anymore, then bring her family to her. Every year. Maybe more than once a year. Family is important to the plaintiff. She should be with her family and we should pay for it.

Use your creativity! What can your number buy the plaintiff? What kinds of experiences? A cruise, yearly trips to Disneyland, movie theater passes, an RV, a vacation home, an addition on her home to move family members in with her, a timeshare, a pro sports team season tickets, passes to the zoo, the opera, you name it! Get to know your plaintiff and the people close to her. Then figure out a way to have your money make a meaningful impact on her life.

3. ANNUAL INCOME

We typically look at the plaintiff's income to understand the value of money to the plaintiff. What is the plaintiff's profession? What was plaintiff's last job? How much money did the plaintiff make per year? What is the plaintiff's lifestyle? We seek out this information in discovery, even when a plaintiff is not advancing a loss-of-income claim. This is because the defense must tie its number for pain and suffering to the impact of money on the plaintiff's life.

In the *Howell* case, I asked the jury to consider the impact of a $100,000 award for pain and suffering. The plaintiff did not work. She was a former school teacher who stopped working about fifteen years before this accident because she didn't like the direction her school was heading. She hadn't held a full-time job since. She had also married a successful plaintiff's lawyer!

I asked the jury to think about how long it would take a teacher to make $100,000. Perhaps several years? Next, I urged the jury to consider how long it would take a teacher to personally save $100,000. Perhaps decades? Perhaps never? I explained to the jury I was not passing judgment on the plaintiff—my mother was a New York City schoolteacher who never earned, let alone saved, $100,000. No, we take the plaintiffs as we find them. One hundred thousand dollars was real money to this plaintiff and would have a meaningful impact on her life.

In discovery, find out how much the plaintiff is making at her job, or her last job. Use this number to ground the jury in reality. Use this number to help the jury come up with a fair and reasonable pain and suffering number for *this* plaintiff. And if you don't find out how much the plaintiff is making, draw a reasonable inference from the facts during closing.

Earlier, I mentioned a recent federal jury trial involving a young boy who suffered serious, life-altering third-degree burns on his entire torso. By the time the case came to trial, he was a young man who had just started his career. He was not making a wage loss claim, so how much he was earning was arguably irrelevant and inadmissible at trial. But we did know where he was working. So, in closing, I asked the jury, "How much does someone working his first job at a Skechers shoe store make? Minimum wage? Twelve dollars an hour? And now, starting out as an entry-level assistant to a dental assistant, how much does that pay? Fifteen dollars an hour? Let's say $30,000 a year. How long does it take for someone making $30,000 a year to earn $500,000 (the number I gave for disfigurement, emotional distress, pain and suffering, etc.)? It would take about 16 years. How much do you think it would take someone making $30,000 a year to save $500,000? It might take a lifetime, right?

Relate whatever dollar amount you are asking the jury to award the plaintiff to her life. Make your money be real. Make it have an impact on the plaintiff and explain that to the jury.

4. INVESTMENT RETURNS

If you are asking the jury to award a big enough number, you should consider making an investment argument in closing. For instance, in the *Howell* case, I argued a $100,000 non-economic damage award would bring the plaintiff a source of comfort and stability for a long time if it was invested. As you may know, the stock market has historically achieved returns of 8 or 9 percent. But if you were to put the money in a savings account right now, you would get only 1 or 2 percent. So let's say you took the $100,000 and invested it at, say, a 5 percent return. The plaintiff would have $5,000 every year. She could use this $5,000 every year to take a special trip to Hawaii with her husband. It would likewise buy a lot of surfboards, surfboard wax, or gas to drive every day to go surfing.

A big deal should be made out of the fact that the principal investment, in this case, $100,000, will be a source of comfort to the plaintiff. If a plaintiff expresses fears about what impact a future surgery or job loss might have on him financially, remind the jury that he still has $100,000 in the bank. So, when the plaintiff wakes up at night worried about providing for his family or paying his mortgage, he will remember he has a sizeable safety net. That $100,000 will allow the plaintiff to rest easy at night with the peace of mind he deserves.

WHAT HAPPENED?

So what happened in the trial where the only issue was non-economic damages? How did we argue the impact of the accident on this semi-professional surfer's life? How did we argue the value of money to the plaintiff, who was the wife of a very successful attorney? How did we respond to the plaintiff's attorney's $100,000-a-screw argument, or his personal attacks on us and our cars? Well, you will have to read the next chapter on addressing a plaintiff's pain and suffering arguments to find out.

CHAPTER 5

DEFEAT PLAINTIFFS' PAIN AND SUFFERING ARGUMENTS

"PLAINTIFF'S COUNSEL IS ONTO us. They know our arguments for pain and suffering. They know how we defuse anger. They know our responsibility story. They know our themes."

I hear this from my attorneys all the time. They are worried plaintiff's counsel know our arguments and strategy. My attorneys are worried they will tell the judge or tell the jury our approach to winning jury trials. My response? So what?

I don't care if the plaintiff's attorney knows every word that is going to come out of my mouth in a trial. They are "onto us" for one reason, and one reason only: because what we are doing to avoid runaway jury verdicts works. What we're doing is fair, legal, and makes sense.

The plaintiff's bar is onto *us*, not anyone else. They are not reading some other defense firm's closing arguments to understand their approach to pain and suffering. They are reading our trial transcripts! No other defense firm in America has our approach to achieving fair and reasonable non-economic damage awards. Ask them. There is nothing for the plaintiff to be "onto" with other defense firms. In fact, plaintiff's attorneys have created a whole industry, a whole movement, of runaway jury verdicts, based solely on the principle that defense lawyers will keep trying cases the same way they always have.

I say so what, because *we* are onto *them*! We know what they're doing. We know how they are manipulating juries across the country. We have a plan to expose and beat them, and this is how we do it.

HOW DO YOU COUNTER PLAINTIFF'S PAIN AND SUFFERING ARGUMENTS?

Keep your friends close and your enemies closer. This is very true in trial work. In addition to using the TM Methods for arguing pain and suffering discussed in the previous chapter, you must be prepared to respond to all the different ways plaintiff's attorneys argue for big non-economic damages. You must know their methods. You must read their books. You must read their closing arguments and their articles and blogs and websites—anything you can get your hands on.

I read closing arguments from big jury trials all the time. It's a little geeky, definitely time consuming, and they can be pretty upsetting. But they really help explain not only why juries give such huge awards, but how plaintiff's attorneys manipulate jurors to reach those results. You will see patterns. But, more importantly, you must figure out what you would have done differently if you were giving the defense's closing argument. This chapter explains what you must do when you stand up to defeat the plaintiff's arguments for non-economic damages.

While plaintiffs have some very effective means for arguing damages, there are only a few ways they do it. The top three methods are: Answer a want ad; break down the total pain and suffering number into days, hours, minutes, and seconds; and put a dollar amount on each element of the pain-and-suffering jury instruction.

There is a new movement afoot, as well. Plaintiff's attorneys across the country are using a fourth way to get large verdicts: by getting jurors to think about expensive things during deliberations. This includes celebrities' incomes and priceless pieces of art. We will discuss how to respond when plaintiff's counsel tells the jury stories about million-dollar works of art or expensive machinery.

ANSWER AN AD

The "answer an ad" approach to arguing pain and suffering can take many forms. The basic premise is to try to get the jury to put themselves in the plaintiff's shoes. Of course this is illegal in most states as it is a variation of the impermissible Golden Rule argument. Most states prohibit plaintiff's attorneys from asking the jury how much money they would want to suffer the same injuries as the plaintiff. It's not a fair question. The jury is there to put a value on the plaintiff's pain and suffering, not their own. It's extremely prejudicial to the defense, and that's why plaintiff's attorneys are always looking for a way around it. (Defense attorneys could learn a thing or two from this never-give-up approach.)

The traditional approach is to ask the jury to imagine a want ad in the newspaper. It's an ad for a job that reads: One day you are driving down the street, passing through an intersection, when all of a sudden a meat truck blows through a red light and slams into your car. Your car is spun around and you are thrown violently to and fro. The pain is immediate and life changing. You will never be the same. You will need three back surgeries. You will be in pain every day for the rest of your life. Your relationship with your loving husband will change. Your carefree, loving personality will be gone. You will not be as strong of a person as you used to be. Most importantly, you will not be able to follow your passion. Your dreams will be cut short because of debilitating pain and physical limitations. You will lose the very essence of who you are.

How much would you want to take this job? Would it be $20 million to take a job where your life would be changed forever? What about $30 million to never be able to follow your passion?

This can be a very effective argument. It's not only done as a want ad. It can be done as a question. For instance, what is the value of having a person's life changed forever? And then explain in detail how this person's life was changed. There are many different ways to present this to a jury, and all of them can be fairly persuasive.

So how do you combat the want ad approach? First, you must address it head on. Ask the jury if they've ever heard of truth in advertising. What does truth in advertising mean? It means advertisers should tell the truth! Is the advertiser telling you the truth in this case? No. If counsel were being truthful, the ad wouldn't read the way he just described, would it? Then explain what the plaintiff's life is really like. Tell the jury the other side of this story.

How else can you respond to the want ad argument? You get real. Tell the jury that this example by plaintiff's counsel isn't fair. No one took out a want ad. This was an accident! We didn't do this on purpose. We didn't take out an ad that the plaintiff answered. No, it was an accident. A mistake. I wouldn't wish it upon my loved ones; I wouldn't wish it upon the plaintiff. No one would. Tell jurors to to ask themselves: why would an officer of the court even make this up? Is he trying to play with their emotions? Is he trying to get them mad? Tell jurors, "I'm sure as an officer of the court, when counsel stands before you in rebuttal, he will admit he was trying to appeal to your emotions and the law strictly prohibits you from allowing bias, sympathy, or prejudice into your deliberations."

First approach by plaintiff's counsel defeated.

MULTIPLES OF TIME

The second approach is to get the jury think about the pain and suffering the plantiff has experienced in terms of minutes, hours, or days and then multiply that time by a small dollar amount. For example, plaintiff's counsel will ask the jury whether being in the kind of pain the plaintiff is experiencing every day would it be worth $100 an hour. What about $50 an hour? How about minimum wage? Would it be worth $12 an hour to have your life changed forever, be in constant pain, not be able to spend time with your family and friends, to be depressed and no longer able to follow your passion? Do you think you should at least get minimum wage for this tragic life? If so, that comes out to 20 cents a minute. Less than a penny a second to never be the person you were before this accident. When you add this up for the next forty years of the thirty-nine-year-old plaintiff's life, $12 an hour, times twenty-four hours a day, times 365 days a year, comes to $4,204,800. Sure, it's a big number, but is it worth less than a penny for even a second to have your life changed forever?

Not a bad approach. Twenty cents a minute seems like nothing. But when you multiply it by how long the plaintiff will likely live, the number can be extraordinary. So what do you do? You could just ignore it, which is how most defense counsel approaches it. I suggest the following response:

"Let me briefly talk about plaintiff's counsel's days, hours, minutes formula. I am not even going to address all of the things that are wrong with his made-up formula. You have already figured out many of the flaws in his scenario, like the fact the plaintiff has already testified he has good days and bad days, not all bad, every second of every day. And what about sleep? Is the plaintiff really in pain 24/7, even while sleeping? Or is this just another exaggeration by plaintiff's counsel to try to trick you?"

"Even more importantly, the law states there is no 'fixed standard' for calculating pain and suffering. There is no formula. You must be very wary of any suggested calculations for pain and suffering by plaintiff's counsel, because applying a fixed standard is against the law."

Bam! Done. They have never responded to this approach in their rebuttal. Because it's fair, it's the law, and it works.

Now there's been a more recent twist to this argument by creative plaintiff's attorneys. Recently they have tried to equate a plaintiff's pain and suffering with the income of the defense experts. Plaintiff's counsel will tell the jury how much defense experts charge by the hour. He will tell the jury how much your experts made on this case. He will try to get in front of the jury how much your expert made last year doing expert work—and, even better, how much the expert made in his career. One radiologist in Los Angeles recently admitted in trial he has made about $30 million over the course of his career doing expert work. Plaintiff's counsel argued, successfully that his client's pain and suffering was at least worth what this defense expert was charging for his opinions about pain.

Another Los Angeles plaintiff's attorney argued that the plaintiff should get at least the hourly rate of the defense expert. The defense expert was making $800 an hour. "How about just $800 a day?" he asked. The actuary tables show the plaintiff will live for 22,000 more days. That comes out to $17.6 million for future pain and suffering if you award the plaintiff only a fraction of what the defense expert gets paid for each day of work. The jury awarded $15 million in that trial, most of it for pain and suffering.

Again, these appear to be somewhat compelling, and maybe even reasonable, arguments for large non-economic damage awards. They are not! How do you convince the jury of that? Well, first of all, fight the urge to do what the well-known defense lawyer did in the $15 million case: he didn't even mention it! You must address it. Call it out to the jury. Ask the jury why on earth the plaintiff's lawyer would be talking about how much a doctor who was in school and training for over twenty-five years makes when the issue is the value of the plaintiff's loss? How much someone who's never met the plaintiff makes a year has nothing to do with the amount of pain the plaintiff has suffered. There is no connection whatsoever.

So why would plaintiff's counsel tell this story? There can be only one reason, and I think you know what that is. The attorney is playing to jurors' emotions. He wants them to make an award not based on sound reason and fairness; he wants them to make an emotional decision. Don't allow it!

Is this a little aggressive? Remember, the good plaintiff's counsel will be going at you and your witnesses the whole closing argument. Why? Because it works. And it works both ways. Be aggressive. Hold plaintiff's counsel accountable for his improper emotional pleas. Also point out to the jury that it sounds like a formula, an impermissible fixed standard, to apply to non-economic damages. I will talk more about our formula argument next.

BREAKING DOWN ELEMENTS OF PAIN AND SUFFERING

The second widely used approach by plaintiff's attorneys to argue non-economic damages is to list the different elements of the plantiff's pain and suffering in the jury instructions and put dollar amounts on each. In California, there are ten possible categories of pain and suffering for which an injured plaintiff may seek compensation. They are set forth in CACI 3905A:

> Past and future physical pain / mental suffering / loss of enjoyment of life / disfigurement / physical impairment / inconvenience / grief / anxiety / humiliation / emotional distress

Plaintiff's counsel will go through every element and tell jurors how much they should award for each. Of course not all elements will apply, but plaintiff's counsel will argue for as many as he can. For nine or ten elements, the number can be pretty substantial. But remember, the amounts he puts up will be double that. Plaintiff's counsel will be presenting to the jury eighteen or twenty different numbers because he's asking for both past and future pain and suffering.

An example argument by plaintiff's counsel might look like this:

Let's take a look at the law on the issue of pain and suffering. The law says that if the evidence supports it, you must award my client for each of these ten elements I have up on the board. Let's go through these different elements. First, physical pain. You've heard a lot of testimony about the pain my client has endured because of this accident. It started immediately, three years ago. You have not only heard from him, but you have heard from his family and his friends about how this has changed my client's life forever. How he was unable to get out of bed for weeks, or work. What is that pain worth, for the last three years? I mean you heard it, you saw the photos, and they were gruesome, and they were real. Just like my client's pain. I suggest to you that to endure that kind of life-changing pain, it would be at least $1 million. You can of course award more.

But that was just the past physical pain. My client's pain is not nearly over. In fact, you heard from expert Dr. Smith that my client's pain may actually get worse over time and may never get better, even with the recommended future surgeries. As you know, the actuary tables indicate my client will live for another thirty-eight years. Over these thirty-eight years, his pain will get worse, every day. So if the past three years are worth $1 million and, again, you are free to award more, then what are the next thirty-eight years of my client's life worth? $38 million? More? Less? Well, I do not think it's worth quite that much, but I do know that the pain my client will endure for the next thirty-eight years of his life will be worse than the last three. So he clearly should be awarded much more than the $1 million of harm he sustained in the past. I respectfully suggest to you a fair and reasonable number for pain and suffering is at least $10 million.

This is just one example of one element of pain and suffering. All ten items will be listed on a board or projected on a screen with two columns next to each. One column will be labeled "Past" and the other "Future." You could have a total of twenty numbers displayed to the jury. Counsel will go through each and admit some do not apply in the case, like maybe disfigurement, for instance, but most do apply. When you add up ten to twenty numbers, the total for non-economic damages can be substantial.

So the jury is feverishly writing down the plaintiff's ten to twenty elements of pain and suffering. This is not good. It's now your turn to deliver your closing argument. What do you do when you stand up? You could hope the jury can't add and just ignore it. Probably not a wise move, especially since the jury can request a calculator.

You do exactly what we have been discussing this whole book: embrace the awkward. Address the toughest parts of your case. Talk to the jury about money. Explain why the plaintiff's arguments are flawed and ridiculous. In this case, point out there is no "must" when it comes to any of these elements. The law does not say the jury "must" make an award for each element. Don't let plaintiff's counsel bully you into awarding him and his client money. What you award the plaintiff for non-economic damages, if anything, is up to the jury, not some plaintiff's lawyer.

Ask jurors to think about why the plaintiff's lawyer would present his damages request like this. He wants there to be a lot of numbers up there. He wants the jury to award a big number. And to get there, he wants them to use a formula. Remember the law—there is no "fixed standard" for calculating pain and suffering. Remind jurors of this, and then address his next argument.

STEALTH BOMBER AND KIM KARDASHIAN

Plaintiff's attorneys also try to get the jury thinking about big numbers by giving them examples of expensive pieces of artwork, or salaries of celebrities or sports stars, or expensive machinery like a stealth bomber. They combine these big-ticket items with compelling stories. Like the Louvre is on fire in Paris and a security guard is told to run into the building and save the *Mona Lisa*. But when he runs into the burning, smoke-filled building, he sees a small child choking to death under the $150 million painting. Without hesitation, the security guard rushes past the priceless art and scoops up the dying child. Why? Because we as a society value human life even more than a $150 million painting. And this decedent was obviously much more important to her family than some old painting. This family deserves much more than a $150 million painting.

Or: a stealth bomber costs a billion dollars to engineer and build. It's a marvel of science and technology. But if the stealth bomber is going to crash, do we save the plane or do we save the pilot? The pilot, of course! Why? Because we value life even more than a billion-dollar marvel of science. This plaintiff, like that stealth bomber pilot, is worth more than a piece of equipment. These can be some pretty moving arguments.

So what do you do? Ask the jury why on earth plaintiff's counsel would even bring this up. Did we hear any evidence of the *Mona Lisa* or Kobe Bryant in the trial? Tell them what he's doing. He wants them to get angry. He wants the jury to not think about what a dollar is worth outside the courthouse. He wants the jury to think it's fake money, like the kind of money the Kardashians or other social-media influencers make. He doesn't want jurors to look at the plaintiff's life. He wants them to think about things that have nothing to do with this trial, hoping they will not come up with a fair and reasonable number as required by law.

OVERCOMING OBJECTIONS TO PAIN AND SUFFERING ARGUMENTS

I have never received an objection to the TM Method for arguing pain and suffering. The arguments I set forth in the preceding chapter are in no way objectionable. Remember, our two-pronged approach to arguing pain and suffering is very simple: what was the impact of this accident on the plaintiff's life and what is the impact of money on the plaintiff.

So why on earth might you receive an objection? Because it works! Also, because plaintiff's counsel knows it's fair. It's certainly more fair than the plaintiff's pain and suffering arguments. Plaintiff's counsel may argue it's improper for the defense to say what the plaintiff would do with any award the jury may give her. It would likely be objectionable for plaintiff's counsel to stand up and say, "If you award my client $1 million, she will give it all to charity." So what do you do if plaintiff's counsel objects to our pain and suffering method?

First of all, we're not telling the jury what the plaintiff will do with the money. We have no idea. We are talking about the value of money to the plaintiff. What impact does money have on this plaintiff's life. We don't care how the plaintiff will spend the money; we are looking at what the plaintiff has used money for in the past. We take the plaintiff as we find her. How she spends money and enjoys her life is how we find her. It is relevant. It is certainly more relevant than the *Mona Lisa*!

Next, assume the objection is sustained and you can't use this method. Of course follow and respect the court's ruling after you've made a clear record. But are you stuck? Do you stop arguing pain and suffering and go onto something else? Do you stop fighting for justice? Of course not!

You must pivot. You must come at this from a different, but fair and reasonable, approach, supported by the law. Try the following, if necessary, during closing argument:

> Let me change gears here for a minute. Let's talk about money. The idea of money. Money itself does nothing for us, right? Putting a dollar bill in our hand or 500,000 of them doesn't make you better, right? The physical receipt of dollar bills in your hand does not help with physical pain or anxiety. No, it is what you can do with money that helps you get back some of that inconvenience and mental suffering you have experienced. I am in no way saying what the plaintiff will do with the money you decide is fair and reasonable in this case. What I am talking about is how $500,000 will have a real impact on the plaintiff's life. I am talking about how $500,000 will impact the plaintiff's physical pain, her mental suffering, her loss of enjoyment of life, and all of the other elements of non-economic damages plaintiff's counsel just wrote on the board for you. I am talking about how $500,000 will allow the plain-

tiff to spend time with her family, and how she misses that, and she needs that, and how we should pay for that. $500,000 is real money to this plaintiff. It will afford her real things to address the real harms she has suffered. It will fly her family to visit with her every year, for the rest of her life. It will pay for real hotels and real vacations. It will make a real difference in her life.

Hopefully that works. What if it doesn't? What if plaintiff's counsel objects again and the judge rules again that you cannot use this method? Do you give up? Of course not! Try this:

Ladies and gentlemen of the jury, let me change gears again. Let me ask you a question: What on earth do the salaries of the Kardashians or of professional athletes have to do with this case? What does the *Mona Lisa* or a stealth bomber have to do with this plaintiff? Did we hear anything about the plaintiff being a pilot or an art collector in the past month of trial? Ask yourselves, why on earth would plaintiff's counsel be asking you to think about huge salaries or art worth millions of dollars? Why wouldn't plaintiff's counsel be talking about evidence? Why wouldn't he be talking about what impact money would have on his client's life? Why is he talking about how much Kobe Bryant is making? What on earth does that have to do with what you guys are trying to decide in this case? Why not talk about bringing this family together. How they can spend time together.

Why would plaintiff's counsel ask you guys to think about all kinds of things that have nothing to do with this case? He would do it for one reason and one reason only, to appeal to your emotions! I'm sure when counsel gets up here in rebuttal, since he is an officer of the court, he will tell you that you must not allow bias, sympathy, or prejudice to enter into your deliberations. They have no place here. I am sure he will admit that $500,000 is real money to the plaintiff. He will discuss the evidence, not some painting, and agree that $500,000 does allow the plaintiff to spend time with her family. It does allow the family to fly to California to visit the plaintiff and stay in hotels, and, most importantly, spend time together. If you listened to the evidence about the plaintiff's life over the last month, you know that $500,000 is real money to this plaintiff. It gives the plaintiff a real chance to start to heal with the support of her loved ones and be on the road to recovery. And she deserves that.

Again, you should never receive any objections to these non-economic damages arguments. I never have in the last 30 years. They are fair and grounded in evidence. If you do receive objections, you are now armed to proceed onward.

WHAT IF THE PLAINTIFF IS RICH?

I'm often asked how to make these arguments if the plaintiff is wealthy. Your non-economic damages number will have no impact on a rich person. How can you afford to give the plaintiff some of the things she has been enjoying in her life? For example, the plaintiff admits she loves to travel. Every summer she spends a month in the Hamptons before she flies in her private jet to the French Riviera, driving her convertible Ferrari from her private villa to her yacht to the casinos of Monte Carlo. How on earth will you be able to come up with a non-economic damages number to relate to this ultra-wealthy plaintiff?

First of all, a jury would hate this plaintiff. I hate her and she isn't even real. Jurors hate rich people. Plaintiff's counsel knows this. They would never allow their client to testify like this. But what if a rich plaintiff testified to enjoying all of the finer things in life? What do you do?

Remember what we discussed about camping? Yes, camping and the South of France are the same thing. Sort of. What they both have in common is shared experiences. Think about it: No one wants to spend a month-long vacation alone. No one wants to drive around in a convertible every day, alone. No one wants to be on their yacht or in the Hamptons or at the casinos, alone. No. What we truly cherish about all of these well-heeled experiences is sharing them with the people we love. So whether you are camping or sipping wine on your Tuscany estate, what you truly enjoy and would miss the most is sharing these times with the people you care about.

If you have a rich plaintiff who admits it on the stand, do the same thing you would do with a camper. Use your creativity to give the plaintiff some of the joy and shared experiences she has been missing since her accident. Explain how your number can do this for the plaintiff. Bring her family and friends to her, not in a private jet, of course! It may be a little more challenging than a typical plaintiff, but it can be done.

QUESTIONS TO ASK IN DISCOVERY

My lawyers are often the ones asking the odd questions at the end of a plaintiff's deposition—the questions that make co-counsel shudder and leave most defense lawyers scratching their heads, at best. The deposition is just about wrapped up and we start asking bizarre questions about the plaintiff's "passion" and what she likes to do for fun. Our co-counsel, and plaintiff's counsel, think we are just building up the plaintiff's case. But on the contrary!

You must find out who this plaintiff really is. What is her passion? What makes her tick? What did she truly enjoy doing in life before this incident? What does she believe our client took from her? And, very often, it's not a plaintiff's job that defines her. It's being a mom, or an artist, or a volunteer, or a mentor, or a musician, or a shopper, or a crafter, or a technology nut, or a sports enthusiast, or church-goer, or anything but her 9-to-5 job. You better know who the plaintiff really is, or you will get killed by the best plaintiff's lawyers.

And you better find this out before trial, because if you don't, you may get hit very hard. The good plaintiff's lawyers will acknowledge their client's job loss, but will say this case is about so much more than just not being able to work. The economic damages in this case are so much smaller than the plaintiff's true loss. This case is about the plaintiff losing the very essence of who she is. Well you better know who that plaintiff is!

So what kind of questions should you ask the plaintiff in deposition to address non-economic damages? Below is our outline of pain and suffering questions we think should be asked in every plaintiff's deposition, in every case:

BEFORE YOU END THE DEPOSITION, MAKE SURE YOU CAN ANSWER THESE TWO QUESTIONS IN A FAVORABLE WAY:

1. What is the impact of the accident on the plaintiff's life— what is the plaintiff's life really like after the accident?
2. What is the impact of money on the plaintiff's life—what is the value of money to the plaintiff?

YOUR QUESTIONS:

You are seeking monetary damages, correct?

> How much for:
> > Medical bills
> > Pain and suffering / non-economic damages

Any other damages for which you are seeking money?

Any other expenses related to the accident or treatment?

List all the ways your life has changed since the accident.
> How did it affect you emotionally?

Have you taken any vacations or trips since the accident?
> Have you gone to any amusement parks?
> Have you been to any live shows?
> Have you taken any weekend trips?
> Have you been to any sporting events?
> Where do you traditionally go for vacation?
> With whom?

What is your passion?
> What are your hobbies?
> What do you like to do for fun?
> How much does this hobby, passion, or fun cost?
> What do you spend money on for enjoyment?

How much money do you make a year?

Did the accident cause you any other financial hardships?

Do you own your home?

What worries you most about your recovery from this accident? (Kids' college tuition, car payment, mortgage payment, taking care of aging parents, retirement?)

Does anything keep you up at night because of this accident?

Why did you file the lawsuit?
> What do you hope to get out of this lawsuit?
> When did you first talk to a lawyer about this incident?

> Was there any particular change to your lifestyle that prompted you to get help from a lawyer?

Do you believe any other party is liable for this accident?
Do you feel like you have been getting better since the accident?
> Do you feel like you will get better in the future?

Remember, most of these questions are supported by the law. Have the jury instruction on pain and suffering available to you during the deposition. Support your questions with the law. For instance, "Is there anything else that keeps you up at night?" If plaintiff's counsel objects to this as irrelevant and overbroad, explain that it's your understanding the deponent is seeking money for mental suffering, anxiety, and loss of enjoyment of life. You are just trying to understand if there is anything that keeps the plaintiff up at night, or causes him anxiety. If plaintiff's counsel does not let his client answer these questions, he should not be able to talk about it at trial, and there will therefore be no non-economic damages or nuclear verdict!

HOW DOES IT ALL END?

So what happens when you really argue pain and suffering? What happens when you talk to the jury about the impact of the accident on the plaintiff and the impact of money on the plaintiff? Well, in the *Howell* jury trial that I mentioned in the prior chapter, good things happened. The president of the Gerry Spence Trial Lawyer's College had asked the jury for almost

$3 million for pain and suffering. He had given an impassioned closing argument. When he was finished, $3 million seemed like a real possibility.

So what did I do? I argued the heck out of damages. First, I had already given our damages number to the jury long before closing argument. It was no surprise that we were seeking a much lower number than plaintiff's counsel. Second, I had to justify our number to the jury in closing argument. I told jurors they must use their judgment and common sense to award a reasonable amount based on the evidence. Our number was fair and reasonable, and would have a meaningful impact on the plaintiff's life. I argued the real impact of this accident on the plaintiff and the impact of money on the plaintiff.

In this particular case, I also went a step further. It was a little dangerous. I told the jury I thought it would be unfair to award Mrs. Howell more than $100,000 in pain and suffering. Yes, it would be unfair to her. Because if you did, you would be telling the plaintiff, as well as her friends and family, that you did not believe them—that when they all testified what a strong woman she was, you would be telling them no, she is not. That she really needs much more than a fair and reasonable number to be made whole.

I told them I did believe in her. I believed she was a strong woman and she would overcome the difficulties she was facing. In fact, she reminded me of a great American hero. His nickname was Iron Horse. He held the record for the most consecutive games played in any major sports league: 2,130 games in a row. He was a baseball player for the Yankees before he was stricken by a terminal illness called amyotrophic lateral sclerosis, or ALS. This disease, which struck down this great American hero, ultimately took his name and today is called Lou Gehrig's disease. The plaintiff reminded me of this hero, I told jurors, and I read to them a portion of his farewell speech given to a sold-out crowd at Yankee Stadium. Fitting for this great American hero, it was on July 4, 1939:

> Fans, for the past two weeks, you have been reading about the bad break I got. Yet today I consider myself the luckiest man on the face of this earth. I have been in ballparks for seventeen years and have never received anything but kindness and encouragement from you fans.
>
> When you have a wonderful mother-in-law who takes sides with you in squabbles with her own daughter—that's something. When you have a father and a mother who work all their lives so you can have an education and build your body—it's a blessing. *(I pointed to the plaintiff's father who was in the audience during closing.)* When you have a wife who has been a tower of strength and shown more courage than you dreamed existed—that's the finest I know. *(I point to Mrs. Howell's husband who was there every day of trial.)*
>
> So I close in saying that I may have had a tough break, but I have an awful lot to live for.

That was Lou Gehrig. I told jurors that I saw the same strength in the plaintiff. I told them they must have seen it, too, over the last three weeks. I told jurors that if they awarded her more than $100,000, they were telling her they don't believe her or her family and friends. "She is a strong woman," I told jurors. And I explained that $100,000 was a fair and reasonable award for her injuries.

This last approach was dangerous. It could certainly have backfired. It may not work for all defense counsel, in all cases.

But it worked in this case. The jury, fortunately, saw it our way and awarded only $690,000, including $340,000 in stipulated economic damages and $350,000 for past and future pain and suffering. The plaintiff had undergone three surgeries and it was undisputed she would need another neck fusion in the next five years. The non-economic damages award was well below the defendant's policy limits and the millions of dollars sought by plaintiff's counsel. This was with no defenses, no experts, no witnesses, and no evidence. We only had the Tyson & Mendes Method for arguing damages. And it worked!

You must be creative, especially in closing argument. Don't just read the jury the law. Don't just tell them the award must be fair and reasonable. Show them. Tell them a story—a story that will move them to action. Use the Tyson & Mendes Method of arguing (1) the real impact of the accident on the plaintiff's life and (2) the impact of money on the plaintiff's life. Show the jury you care about the plaintiff. Explain how your number will have a positive affect on her life. Use these methods in every jury trial, and I guarantee you will avoid runaway jury verdicts.

CHAPTER 6

THE VALUE OF A LIFE

This is the chapter I hesitated to write. Putting a value on a life. Who has the right to do that? Who would want to do that? Can you really put a value on a life? If not impossible, giving a life a dollar figure sounds, at best, cold and heartless—especially coming from a defense lawyer.

But if you try enough cases, you will try a wrongful death case. And if you do try a death case, you will have to give the jury your opinion on a lost loved one's value. It's not easy. So, rather than sugarcoat this topic or present you with an example of a case I tried where I represented the ideal defendant—remorseful, contrite, a good person who simply made a bad mistake—I am going to share what it's like to defend the unforgivable.

THE CASE

"Do you think I should ask for zero?" That was the question I asked my associate more than 10 years ago, the night before I was to give my closing argument in a tragic wrongful death case.

"Ask the jury to award no money for the value of this young girl's life? I don't know about that Bob. Seems pretty risky to me," my associate responded.

He was right, of course. This was a bad case. The jury had to be very angry at my teenage client for what he did to his friends that night.

Not far from the motel where I was staying in Merced, California, my client killed two of his friends and one unborn baby. He was drunk and high on methamphetamine, speeding down a one lane country road late at night. While driving over ninety miles an hour, he lost control of his vehicle and rolled it into a drainage ditch.

How could this have happened? Well, it was about 4 a.m. My client, a nineteen-year-old named Juan, was asleep in the back of a car in central California. It had been a long night for him and his three young friends. The stars were out, in full glimmering glory. The air was cool and moist and blowing through the cracked open windows of their old four-door sedan. It was a perfect evening for a drive.

But my client was not aware of any of this; he was exhausted. He was lying spread out on the back seat, sleeping hard.

These youth were in the breadbasket of California, the Central Valley, about 300 miles north of Los Angeles and 100 miles south of Sacramento. Farmland as far as the eye could see. Almonds, tomatoes, corn, cattle. This was the land of hardworking farmers and migrants, who worked the fields by day and spent time with family at night. Merced was a rural town of people who valued the American Dream. A place like many others in America, where if you worked hard and tried your best, you might create a better life for your children and their children.

But, sometimes, these values aren't immediately passed down. Sometimes, in a small town, young adults can stray from what's right. They get bored. They want to do something fun. This was one such night.

And on this night, hopes and dreams were shattered. Two teenagers and an unborn baby were dead. This was truly a wrongful death.

Boredom led three young people: Juan; his best friend, Mr. Gonzalez; and their friend, Rosie, down a path that would change their lives, and the lives of many others, forever. Juan was driving. It was Mr. Gonzalez's parents' car. Earlier that night, they had snuck into seventeen-year-old Gonzalez's parents' bedroom and taken the car keys. Mr. Gonzalez's parents did the right thing: they called the police on their son and told them he'd stolen the car. But it was too late.

The bored teenagers found drugs and alcohol. And although my client was asleep and had no desire to drive, when awoken, he did just that. He had no recollection of speeding, or losing control of the steering wheel, or rolling over several times into a ditch, and certainly no memory of seeing his two friends dead in a ravine.

So why on earth was I discussing with my associate years later whether I should ask the jury to return a verdict of zero dollars for the life of a sixteen-year-old girl and her unborn baby? The plaintiff's counsel had already let the jury know he would be asking for $10 million, plus a significant sum for punitive damages to punish my client for his reprehensible behavior. It was not an unreasonable request by any stretch.

We had no defense. My client had already been convicted of manslaughter. In fact, he had been released from jail shortly before this civil trial. But he was not remorseful. After meeting him, I asked him to wear only long-sleeved shirts to trial. He had apparently joined a gang while in prison and had quite a few tattoos.

During trial, a police officer testified that this was one of the worst accidents he had ever investigated. He was literally just about off the stand when plaintiff's counsel had a *Colombo* moment: "Is there anything else you remember about this accident?"

The police officer paused, looked at my client, and said, "Yes. The defendant acted as if he could care less he had just killed two of his friends." You could see the shock, the anger, in the jurors' faces as they turned to glare at my client. My client, who only days before had to be persuaded to even accept liability in this trial. He did not want to take responsibility for killing his friends, even though he was driving the only car on the road. Remember, he was asleep in the back seat when his friends woke him and made him drive. He certainly didn't want to say he was sorry.

So how do you even think of asking a jury to award no money at all to a mom who lost her sixteen-year-old daughter and unborn grandchild? First, let's talk about how you discuss the value of a life.

PRESENT THE TRUTHS

First, you must do everything we have discussed in this book, and more. You must recognize, acknowledge, and show compassion for those involved in the case. You must be aware of what will make the jury angry towards your client and his actions. And you must embrace and defuse that anger by accepting sincere responsibility, and maybe liability, where appropriate.

You cannot pretend to care—you must really care. Sincere compassion is critical. As a defense attorney, you must present the best possible defense for your client, but that does not mean you are void of sympathy or even disgust over what has happened. Loved ones have lost a family member. This should unequivocally engender a conciliatory and humbled approach on your part.

Humanize your client. If possible, show your client cares. Present the type of person he was before and after the incident. Share how this event has impacted him. What current and future value does this person offer to his own family and community? If your client is a business, why does it exist? What good does this business do? What value does it add to the community? Who makes up this company? Who are the people, the everyday fellow citizens, who are this company? Tell their story.

What else do you do in a wrongful death case? You embrace the awkward. Someone died. Whether it was your client's fault or not, it happened and you better acknowledge it, in a real, considerate, and, yes, caring way. Acknowledge the loss. Acknowledge the raw emotion people are experiencing. Better yet, share the emotions you're personally experiencing about being tasked to address the unthinkable and put a value on a life. This is hard. Of course it's nothing like what this family has gone through, but it is hard for you, too. If a jury sees you are truly emotionally invested in this case, they will be more receptive to what you have to say.

Ultimately, you have to come up with a number. And you have to give that number to the jury. And once you provide that number, you must own it. Give jurors this number early and often. Let them know this is an extremely difficult thing for them to do. It is difficult for you to do. But you must share it with confidence and conviction. Mention the number in voir dire, opening, and closing. Work it in with witnesses. Make it part of the theme of your defense.

IDENTIFY A NUMBER

It's the goal of the plaintiff's attorney to assign the highest possible value to the decedent's life, often much higher than they believe any reasonable jury would award. And they often have emotion and sympathy on their side. But that is not enough for them. Good plaintiff lawyers will tell the jury stories to get them thinking of large numbers. They will often use the salaries of sports stars from the city where the case is tried.

One such story is about Kobe Bryant. A plaintiff's lawyer will tell the jury that Kobe Bryant earned $30 million a year to play basketball. And if you ask his teammates and the organization if he was worth it, they would say definitely. Kobe was so much more to his team than just a player who shot baskets or excelled at defense. Kobe was the glue that kept the team together. He raised everyone's game around him. He was the star of the team and without him, they would not have won all of those championships. To his teammates, Kobe was worth every dime of his salary. Well, a plantiff's attorney will argue, the decedent in this case was the father and husband. He was the Kobe Bryant of his family. He kept them together, he raised them up, he was their rock, he was their star. We as a society value a basketball player at $30 million for dribbling a ball. Isn't this father worth much, much more than $30 million to his family?

It is a moving argument. It has worked many times for plaintiff lawyers across the country. But it is not fair and should never be used in a courtroom. It is not evidence and it is not a reasonable inference from the evidence. Kobe Bryant did not testify in this case; he was never even mentioned. His name is being referenced for one reason only: to stir up the emotions of the jury. You must respond to this argument by pointing out its intent and telling your own story.

Yes, you must have your own explanation for why your number is reasonable. Of course, you must refute the plaintiff's number, but, even more important, you must be able to explain why your dollar amount for a life is fair and reasonable. And while the loss of love, comfort, and society is different than pain and suffering, use the same approach. There are two things that must be considered when you evaluate non-economic damages in a wrongful death case: first, what is the impact of this incident on the plaintiff? And, second, what is the impact of money on the plaintiff?

Arguing non-economic damages in a wrongful death case is more difficult than in an employment case or tort case. The loss is final; it is real, it is forever. It is hard to do this. But your challenge is to get to know the plaintiff. You must understand who the decedent was to them. Who was this family, what were they like? What did they do together? Before trial ever begins, you must find out this information. In depositions, you must ask questions to learn the following:

- What was the deceased's employment status before their passing?
- What role/impact did they have in the lives of their family?
- What is the financial impact of their loss on their family?
- How did the family bond and enjoy each other's company before the accident?
- What exactly did the family do together? How did they spend their time? Where did they vacation?
- What is their fondest memory of the decedent?
- What made them most proud about their dad/mom/son, etc.?
- What do they miss most about the decedent?
- What made the decedent happy? What made the decedent sad?
- What is the plaintiff's biggest disappointment now that the decedent has passed?

Feel uncomfortable asking these questions? Good, you should. This is hard; it is awkward. Are you worried that by asking these questions in deposition, you might be building up the plaintiff's case? You might be giving them ideas about their loss that would never have come up at trial, but for your questions? Stop kidding yourself. These questions and the information they yield is what your entire case is about. This is the core of the loss. It is not the financial loss; anyone can figure that out. It is the human loss. The family loss. The loss of love, comfort, and society. That is the loss. And you better understand it, entirely, before you try to put a number on it. Because that is your next challenge: talk to the jury about the impact of money on the plaintiff's life.

APOLOGIZE, IF APPROPRIATE

There is no art to an apology. There is no orchestrated way to apologize. There is no perfect time to apologize. There is no strategy to an apology. There are no special words, coming from a particular witness or from you. No, there is only one way to apologize in a jury trial: Only if you mean it. Let me be clear, only apologize in a trial if you really are sorry for what happened to the plaintiff. No exceptions.

Anything less than a heartfelt, honest apology will be hollow. It will not be effective and it will negatively impact your credibility with the jury. Being yourself and being truthful is critical. If you or your client are not sorry, don't say it. Don't practice it so it sounds sincere. Don't try to time it just right. Don't work on your word choice. Just don't say it at all, unless you mean it.

An insincere apology is always worse than no apology at all. For example, as I'm writing this book, the Johnson & Johnson talcum powder cases are going on—and have been going on for years. The most innocent seeming of products, baby powder, is now alleged to cause all types of horrific illnesses, such as ovarian cancer and mesothelioma. Using what seemed to be a harmless product has, allegedly, been a death sentence for tens of thousands of people.

Prosecuting and defending these cases has become its own little industry, with ads seeking more plaintiffs everywhere you look. The fight over the science behind these claims and the defense of them is fierce. Millions of dollars are being spent to analyze the product and investigate the cause of these diseases. Hundreds of experts, scientists, and researchers are dug in for quite the battle that is playing out in courtrooms across the country. The science is fascinating to many, including defense lawyers.

But this is not a fight for science or medicine. This is not even a fight for right or wrong. No, this, at the core of it, is a fight for life. These trials are happening in courtrooms, not laboratories. These courtrooms are full of people, not lab rats. These people are real, with real losses and real fears. There are people in these courtrooms literally fighting for their lives and the lives of their loved ones. So while the science and experts and charts and studies are all important parts in the fight, never forget what this war is all about: life.

APOLOGY NOT ACCEPTED

One such battle played out in California recently, where Johnson & Johnson went to trial over its defense that baby powder did not cause a plaintiff's cancer. The case highlighted the power of the word "Sorry."

The husband of the dying plaintiff had just finished testifying on direct exam. It was emotional testimony, to say the least. Tears flowed as he described how his wife's terminal mesothelioma diagnosis had changed his family's lives forever. She was the love of his life and completed him for the last twenty years. She was always the life of the party and made him whole. Now she would not see their daughters graduate high school and would die before year's end. There was not a dry eye in the Oakland courtroom.

It was now the defense lawyer's turn to cross-examine the grieving husband. There is a school of thought among trial attorneys that you ask no questions of the spouse in this instance. He will not be able to prove or disprove whether the plaintiff's mesothelioma was caused by her use of baby powder. He was already very emotional and the last thing you'd want to do is make it worse.

As you would imagine, Johnson & Johnson hired some of the most expensive trial lawyers in the country, a whole team of Ivy League-educated lawyers, from Am Law 100 firms, to fight till the end. And fight they did. But with the husband on the stand, they made the right decision. The team of lawyers decided to question the husband, briefly. More importantly, they decided to apologize.

The grieving husband had just finished sharing his feelings about his wife's impending death. The defense was going to use this opportunity to apologize. In a very technical trial, with data and reports and medical experts every day, this was a human moment. A real moment. A moment for the defense to show that no matter what caused this woman's terrible, life-ending disease, they cared. The defense recognized this was not a case about lab rats or a scientific study of monkeys in the 1960s. No, this was a trial about real people, with real loss, and real heartache. Here was this very real moment:

"Sir, I just want to say I am very sorry about your wife's diagnosis. Sir, I think I am just going to have two questions ...."

Um, what? Sorry for his wife's "diagnosis"? Are you kidding me? Is that what this man had testified about for the last hour? His wife's "diagnosis," really? Is that what had happened to this family? The mom got a diagnosis? No! The plaintiff was dying from a terminal disease called cancer. It is real, it is awful, and it kills people.

Excuse my language, but either be sorry for this man's unimaginable loss and communicate it effectively and humanely, or sit down and shut the fuck up! Seriously, if this is what you are going to do with a grieving witness, then just sit there and wait for the next scientist to take the stand. Because you are not doing your client any favors. Nope, you are just giving the jury another reason to do what they did to Johnson & Johnson in this case and award $29 million.

Was the defense lawyer really sorry, but his delivery was off? Was this a runaway jury verdict or was it justice? I don't know. But like many large jury verdicts, when you drill down, they are understandable. Maybe even predictable. You see a pattern. A pattern of defense lawyers seeming like they don't care about real tragedies. An insincere apology is another piece of this predictable pattern of nuclear verdicts. Do not do it!

CLOSING

At the end of my wrongful death trial, I did ask the jury to award zero dollars for the value of the sixteen-year-old daughter and her unborn child. It certainly was a big risk, given all of the aggravating factors in this case, and the less-than-desirable defendant. The grief, the agony, the loss was all very real and painfully raw. But I battled my own emotions and shared the truths.

What did the jury do? They awarded $0 to the young woman's mom. They awarded funeral costs, as well as punitive damages, all totaling about $12,000. Nothing was awarded to the mom for the loss of love, comfort, and society. It demonstrated that despite the horrific events, the jury was able to set aside their emotions and address the facts.

I will never know for sure why the jury told the plaintiff the value of her daughter's and unborn granddaughter's lives were zero. But I do know this: it was not because I showed the jury I could care less about the grieving mother. I did care. It was a hard, emotional case to try. At least four jurors were crying while the mom was on the stand. And it was not because I was ever disrespectful or asked heartless, unnecessary questions of mourning witnesses. It was certainly not because we seemed unreasonable to the jury, fighting losing battles and wasting their time while losing credibility. Defense lawyers do this all the time. Fight everything, at all costs. That is the defense mantra. In most cases, when it doesn't work, you simply alienate the jury.

Your job is to be the most reasonable person in the room. This is very important in a wrongful death case, especially the death of a child.

We did advance our themes of responsibility, reasonableness, and common sense with every witness. It took quite a bit of work, but we did personalize our client to the jury. We took responsibility. The jury knew our client went to jail for this crime. No one else in the trial took any responsibility. So we talked about who else might have responsibility. We of course had to deal with these issues in a delicate and compassionate way, but we did have to address them. The plaintiff did not know where her daughter was that evening, that she had gone joyriding with her friends. The mom did not know her daughter was pregnant. The deceased daughter did make a decision to use drugs that night and go speeding around in a stolen car, while pregnant. Again very sensitive issues that must be treated respectfully, but all facts relevant to the loss sustained.

The jury heard all of the evidence and reached a fair and reasonable verdict, as harsh as it may seem. This is the trial I do not talk about with my friends or acquaintances. Unless you were in that courtroom, it's tough to explain why this was a just result. After closing arguments, plaintiff's counsel was not surprised by the verdict. He, of course, was not happy. Okay, he was extremely upset with us, but he understood why it happened. Is this verdict any worse than the multi-million-dollar jury verdicts with no real injuries that plaintiff attorneys brag about all of the time? I don't know. But I know we fought for justice for all, not just the plaintiff. As Aristotle so famously stated, "The law is reason, free from passion."

CHAPTER 7
HAVE A THEME

SOMETIMES TRIAL DOES not go as well as you would like. A witness goes south on you, a judge changes course with her rulings, you do not have the evidence you thought you would, other bad evidence gets introduced, a witness is a no show at trial, or any of the whole host of other things that can happen in a jury trial that are out of your control. The reality is not all trials go well or as planned.

This is one of the reasons you need a theme. You need a message and a story that cannot be derailed by a rogue ruling or one witness' unexpected testimony. You must have a big idea, with a universal belief that transcends any one piece of evidence or other aspect of a trial. A theme that will resonate with a jury, regardless of whatever missteps happen in a trial. Because missteps will happen. And without a unifying, overarching theme for the jury, your trial could be just a series of missteps.

MEXICO V. GERMANY

A few years ago, we were defending an employer in a wrongful termination, harassment, and racial discrimination case. It involved two immigrants: a supervisor originally from Germany forty years ago and an employee from Mexico who had moved to the United States fifteen years earlier. We tried the case about fifteen miles from our Southern border with Mexico, in San Diego. There were some tough issues in the case about race and money. I needed a better theme than plaintiff's counsel, because things sure were stacking up against us.

My clients were rich. There was no hiding it. They lived in one of the nicest suburbs of San Diego called Rancho Santa Fe, the home of many celebrities and the super-rich. Bing Crosby started his Clambake golf tournament there, before the PGA moved to Pebble Beach. The founders of McDonald's and Taco Bell, as well as Howard Hughes, had all lived there. Today, Bill Gates has a home in the exclusive "Covenant" area of Rancho Santa Fe, as well as Jenny Craig, Mike Love of The Beach Boys, Phil Mickelson, and many others. The expression is you can't hide money. In this case, it was true.

My clients were a good-looking couple in their forties. The husband was a very successful real estate developer and apartment owner, and his wife was a horse lover and philanthropist. They lived in a modest (modest for "The Ranch," as it's called) home of about 4,000 square feet. They had no children. They had a maid, Maria who was the plaintiff in this case. Maria was originally born in Mexico and had worked for my clients for about four years. My clients were pleased with her work as their full-time maid.

My clients decided to move into a new home. It was a mansion by any definition. It was approximately 12,000 square feet with horse stables and a riding track. It was a big, beautiful, newer Spanish-style home. It was not only a lot of home for this couple, it was a lot of home for Maria. Even though she worked every day, she struggled to keep the mansion clean. She needed help.

THE FIGHT

My clients hired a house manager to oversee their full-time maid. The new house manager was an older lady with a lot of experience supervising maids and managing big homes. We will call her "Ingrid." Although she had come to America as a young woman, almost forty years ago, Ingrid still had a heavy German accent.

Ingrid was hired to manage Maria and keep the house clean. Maria was not happy with the new house manager. After working for my client for years in a much smaller home, she now had a new boss. Ingrid was strict. She would make Maria get on the ground to see the dirty spots in the corners and floors she had missed. Maria claimed Ingrid would push her head down to the floor and essentially stick her nose in the dirt. Ingrid said she would just point.

Maria claimed Ingrid also constantly berated her about not learning English despite being in the United States for fifteen years. Ingrid admitted she thought Maria should learn English. Ingrid believed all immigrants to America should learn English, just like she did many years ago. She even tried to get Maria to read a book about learning English. Needless to say, it had been a rocky few months for the two employees.

One day the wife came home from tending to her horses to hear her house manager and maid screaming at each other in her TV room. The two had been folding clothes and watching the news. High schools in Los Angeles were staging walkouts in protest of something that was not clear to them. Ingrid admittedly said something about how the kids should be in school learning English. The two began screaming at each other in their native tongues. The wife walked in and separated the two. Maria ran into the laundry room and began kicking and punching the washing machine. When the wife tried to talk to her, she sat on the dryer and just kept yelling and kicking the dryer.

My client was very upset. When her husband came home that evening, they decided this was not working and that Maria had to go. They fired her the next day. But before they fired her, Maria came to work with a handwritten note in broken English. In her two page letter, Maria explained her side of the story. She explained how she had been harassed and berated by Ingrid for the last six months. She detailed the physical, forceful touching by Ingrid. How Ingrid made her cry most days. How Ingrid threatened to have Maria deported all of the time. She would threaten to call immigration if Maria did not work harder. Ingrid would make racist statements about Mexicans and their intelligence, and the statements were detailed in Maria's letter. These alleged comments by Ingrid were clearly offensive. Two years later, we were in a jury trial.

FROM BAD TO WORSE

This was not a good case to try. On a technical level, you cannot just fire a long-term employee like my clients did. In California, employees have rights, lots of rights. One of these rights is that an employee should be able to come to work and not be harassed and berated for any reason, and certainly not because of their race. And if an employee complains of harassment, an employer must, at the very least, investigate the complaints. The employee definitely should not be fired right after they complain of harassment.

In this case, my clients did nothing to stop the alleged harassment. In fact, they fired their maid the same day they received her complaint of harassment. We were dead to rights on a purely legal basis. And then it only got worse for us when we looked at the bigger issues in the case.

The case was being framed as rich vs. poor. A rich, good-looking couple living in a home that everyone wanted. Plaintiff's counsel made sure jurors saw the home. A hardworking mother, trying to provide for her family, thrown out on the street after years of serving the rich. This case was about race as well. A Hispanic woman was fired by a white couple, after she was harassed by a white German woman for six months. It also involved discrimination over a woman speaking her native language in the face of a boss insisting she speak English.

All of these issues were tough. They were tough to talk about anywhere, let alone to a jury of twelve strangers. But that is what we had to do. We had to address these issues head on. We had to tackle some of the toughest issues facing our society, let alone my clients, all within the constraints of a courtroom. Combined with what appeared to be our clear violations of applicable employment law, this case was a loser. And if a jury got angry, it could be really bad.

So what do you do? First, you better have a theme. And your theme better be good, and better than the plaintiff's theme. Because as I discuss at the end of this chapter, things can go from bad to worse once the trial starts.

WHAT IS A THEME?
A theme tells the bigger story behind a case. It goes beyond the facts and witnesses to paint a picture of what really matters. And when we talk about what matters, we are talking about what matters to the jury. What is important and will resonate with them. What will move them emotionally and rationally to consider the case from your perspective and the perspective of the person you are representing.

Rarely have I seen plaintiff's counsel argue a case without a clear theme. In most cases, the plaintiff's theme is focused more narrowly on the facts and witnesses of the case. And the theme they present is often intended to engender a very specific response. Plaintiff's counsel wants jurors to be angry and to direct that frustration directly at the defendant and the defense counsel. This means they will focus on everything the defendant has done wrong. They will focus on every single misstep. And they will focus on how they are greedy and self-serving. While some of these things may be true and may be a good way to advance their theme, it certainly does not tell the entire story.

The defense wants to address and, whenever possible, counter the plaintiff's accusations. But sometimes that's just not possible. Sometimes what the plaintiff is saying is absolutely true. And remember it's always best to accept responsibility where appropriate. It demonstrates to the jury you are trying to be fair and reasonable. However, even if you're accepting some or all responsibility, or a witness or unexpected facts arise that hurt your case, you should always present a broader theme.

From the defense perspective, your theme must address broader issues in your case that strike a positive chord with jurors. Does your client contribute to the community? Was your client acting in a forthright manner? Was your client acting in good faith to reasonably and responsibly pursue the same liberties and dreams afforded to all people and companies in this country, big or small, rich or poor? A theme gives meaning and context to your facts, to the evidence in a trial. It causes a jury to react in either an emotional way or a thoughtful way, consistent with their belief of the truth, of what really happened. As a defense attorney, it's your job to identify these themes and begin to introduce them from day one.

WHAT WORKS AND WHAT DOESN'T WORK

As you will recall, the core principles I use in every trial are responsibility, reasonableness, and common sense. When trying to introduce or further a theme in a trial, doing so when it is in contrast to one or more of these principles does not work well. Jurors want to do what's right. Moreover, they want you and your client to do what is right. While it is your duty to inform the jury as to what you think is right and why, it starts with you taking the appropriate responsibility for the events that transpired. Anything short of this, or any theme you try to advance that is in opposition of this, will likely hurt your credibility with the jury and will not help you or your client. Remember, accepting some or all responsibility does not mean you are posturing for an unfavorable verdict. It just means you are doing the right thing and simultaneously establishing trust with a jury, which goes a long way to having them ultimately find in your favor.

Likewise, your theme should be reasonable. As a defense attorney, it is expected you are going to offer a different narrative than the plaintiff. But it should not be unreasonable. It should not contradict concrete facts. And it should not be presented in a manner that asks a jury to compromise what they feel is reasonable and fair and just. It is your job to explain to them how and why what you are presenting fits these criteria.

Last, common sense can be your best defense against a mountain of unfavorable witnesses and facts. It may be illegal to jaywalk. There may be signs up telling you the definition of jaywalking and reminding you not to do it. And in addition to countless witnesses and video of you jaywalking, you also accept responsibility for jaywalking. But, if the context within which you jaywalked meets the criteria for common sense in the eyes of the jury, then the jury will accept the indiscretion. Your theme needs to be based in common sense.

BIAS, PASSION, AND PREJUDICE

The law says bias, sympathy, prejudice, or public opinion should not influence the jury's verdict. But this is virtually an impossible task. Every juror who walks into the courtroom comes with some bias, sympathy, and prejudice. It's human nature. It's not politically correct to talk about it, but these biases exist. To expect a jury to be completely free of bias, sympathy, and prejudice is unreasonable. Accordingly, if jurors are going to have these tendencies, they better be in favor of you and your client!

Many believe plaintiffs can easily elicit emotional reactions from bias, passion, and prejudice. To be sure, the best plaintiff's attorneys powerfully sway juror bias to their benefit. They use the reptile theory (discussed in Chapter 9) and other psychological tricks to elicit anger and sympathy in pursuit of big verdicts. When a quadriplegic is wheeled into the courtroom, a young mother dies, a child is left disfigured, or a hardworking couple loses their life's fortune, it's all but impossible for a juror to resist their bias, sympathy, and prejudice. The plaintiff in these traumatic situations definitely have the upper hand on emotion and sympathy. But the defense has just as moving truths that it must share with the jury. We must appeal to these higher values to obtain a verdict that is fair and just, for all.

BIGGER VALUES IN THE COURT ROOM

So how does one make use of higher values? You do this by stating the values. Early. Often. Out loud. It begins with voir dire. Ask jurors whether it is important to be honest, to be honorable, to accept responsibility, to contribute to society, to do the right thing. Ask them how they feel about these values. Are they important to them? Are these values they try to instill in their children? Can they ultimately return a verdict that is fair and reasonable and just?

Appeals to higher values should continue into the opening statement. Personalize your client by telling their story. Demonstrate how they personify the values we all treasure. Discuss the evidence that supports these values.

Advance these values with every witness. Illicit testimony showing how your client lives these values and how the plaintiff may not.

Values should be a central aspect of your closing argument. Honesty. A plaintiff has one obligation when they come to court, to tell the truth. How did the plaintiff fail to meet that obligation in this case? Honor. Honor is coming to court, accepting responsibility, saying "hold me accountable." Justice. Justice is a reasonable verdict based on the evidence.

We frequently litigate against plaintiff's attorneys who like to talk about fighting for justice. They go by names like "the justice team," or "trial lawyers for justice," as if justice was a one-sided "plaintiffs only" value. You are fighting for justice too!

How about justice for the hardworking small business owner, extorted with a meritless ADA lawsuit? Justice for the employer wrongfully accused of misconduct by a vengeful, disgruntled employee? Justice for the accountant scapegoated for the business deal gone wrong? Justice in the face of outrageous, unsubstantiated, predatory demands? We seek a fair and reasonable verdict. The defense must remind the jury of our fight for justice.

The good plaintiff's lawyers tell emotional stories about their lives and try to relate those stories to the case. Plaintiff's attorney Gerry Spence is famous for telling moving stories. Others share a story of overcoming adversity. Some tell Biblical tales, like David and Goliath.

Defense counsel must tell a better story. We must appeal to these higher values.

BIGGER VALUES REFLECTED THE JURY'S VERDICT

Do jurors want to live in an America where people tell the truth, accept responsibility for their actions, work hard, care for one another, are good citizens, and do the right thing? Do they want to live in an America full of healing, hope, and change? Do they want to live in an America where people strive for a better life, to live the American dream—a value embodied by the Statue of Liberty?

Or do jurors want to live in an America where people sue each other to resolve conflicts? Where lawyers refer clients to doctors and doctors refer clients to lawyers? Where the truth is misrepresented? Where people refuse to accept responsibility for their own actions? Where our laws are exploited for profit? And where there is no healing, no hope, and no change?

Ultimately, jurors want to do the right thing. You just need to give them the justification.

TRIAL CAN BE A SERIES OF MISSTEPS

So what happened in my employment trial? It was not going well. The law was against us, the facts were against us, sympathy was against us, and maybe even justice was against us. We darn well better at least have a good theme, because things were about to get worse.

Shortly before trial, we learned my client's wife was not going to be at trial, only the husband. She observed the altercation between her maid Maria and house manager Ingrid. She was very upset by this fighting in her home and convinced her husband to fire Maria. She now was not going to be at trial to tell her story of what happened. Even worse, the jury was going to find out why my client was not at trial. Jurors learned she would be in Florida tending to her show horses and could not fly back for this trial. Yes, the jury was essentially told my client cared more about horses than her Hispanic maid! Not good.

But it got worse. Ingrid, their former German house manager, had retired recently and did not really want to be involved in this trial. We tried to prep her for her testimony, but she was a very stern woman and believed what she believed. So when plaintiff's counsel called her as a witness, we were concerned.

Ingrid initially did okay on the stand, until the subject turned to her belief that everyone who comes to the United States should learn English, just like she did. She admitted she told Maria often that she better learn English. She even offered to help her learn English. Plaintiff's counsel asked Ingrid if she had a book about learning English. Of course she did. She was asked by counsel, "And is this book you have called 'How to Teach your Maid English?'" "Yes it is," replied Ingrid. "And I have it right here." And there it was. This worn out paperback book from the '60s or '70s, yellow pages and all, being pulled out of her purse and pranced in front of the jury by plaintiff's counsel for all to see. Of course Ingrid explained how she had helped many Hispanic maids learn English over the years with this book. The jury was looking at us and I was trying to not look horrified. We knew about the book, but we had no idea she would bring it to court!

FROM BAD TO WORSE

Well at least we still had my client to testify. The expression you can't hide money certainly fit this gentleman. He dressed impeccably, with beautiful sports coats and watches. Everything was first class. At this point, it made no sense to tell him to wear jeans. The jurors already knew he lived with just his wife in a 12,000 -square-foot mansion in the fanciest part of San Diego and the jury had even seen photos of the beautiful estate. The good news is we were able to prepare our client for his testimony. We spent hours with him. Went over and over his testimony. We grilled him and we grilled him again. It was tight.

On the day he testified, he did quite well with us questioning him. He explained he came home to find his wife very upset. He found out Maria and Ingrid had been fighting, and Maria just snapped. Maria was screaming and kicking their washing machine and dryer and could not be consoled. His wife was extremely upset and frightened, in her own home. They both agreed that evening they would fire Maria the next day.

When he saw Maria the next morning she handed him a note. He read the note at work. While he understood the note was complaining of harassment, my client and his wife had already decided the night before to fire her. There was no reason to investigate; their decision was made. He went to work to have his accounting department cut Maria's final check and give it to her when he got home.

Pretty tight. Our direct exam was over. We felt pretty good. Now the cross-exam by plaintiff's counsel. Early questioning went quite well. He was not too defensive. Again, he is an extremely smart businessman and successful CEO of a large real estate company. He could handle this.

The cross-exam seemed to be winding down when plaintiff's counsel asked, "So you decided to fire your maid the night before when you were talking to your wife, right?" "Yes," he replied. "So the next morning when you saw Maria in your home before you left for work, you had already decided you would fire her, right?" "Yes." He was doing fine. Plaintiff's counsel then asked, "Well if you had already decided to fire my client the night before, why didn't you fire her the first thing in the morning when you saw her?"

Oh, this was a softball question. We had gone over this question a bunch of times. The reason he didn't fire her that morning was because he had to have his accounting department figure out the amount of her final check and he would hand her the check. This was easy.

So what did my client say when asked why he didn't fire Maria on the spot that morning when he saw her? "I didn't fire her in the morning because the house was dirty." Um, what?! Did he just say he didn't fire his Hispanic maid in the morning because his house was dirty? He waited to arguably change this lady's life forever because he wanted her to clean his house one more day? Even though she might be getting harassed one more day by the German house manager that she had complained about in writing, my client needed his house cleaned. I swear I heard a gasp come from the jury. They all looked at us. It was bad.

So the law was against us, the evidence was against us, my own client seemed to be against us, what was left? Well we still had our themes.

BIGGER THEMES WORK

In this case, we decided to go with a couple of themes. First we went with the theme of a home. Second, we embraced the awkward and went with the importance of immigration to our country. How did we do it? We did it the same way we always do, we started early and often.

In voir dire, I asked the jury to tell me what the word "home" meant to them. Many of the responses from the potential jurors were awesome. They included words like safe, peace, calm, rest, security, and tranquil. We were trying to convince the jury our homes were different. Different than an office. Different than a large company with a handbook and a risk manager and HR director. A home is place where we should feel safe, not scared of some irate and erratic worker. We worked this sense of peace and security in with several witnesses. We used the jurors, own words throughout the trial to convince them a home was different. Of course it is no different in the eyes of the law. My clients' home was a workplace for a house manager and a maid. The plaintiff had all the same rights of any worker in California. But we had a theme.

Immigration. Yes, as controversial as it is, we tackled the issue of immigration in America. In fact, we made it our theme. We started off in voir dire when I asked them, "What is the national language of our country?" Several of the jurors quickly raised their hands. The first couple of answers were English. I explained that unlike many countries, we have no national language in the United States. We started a discussion about this. I asked people how they felt about this. Did they think everyone should learn English when they live in the United States? There were some strong opinions both ways, which was very important to find out. People discussed that non-English speakers have been coming to this country for centuries and it was these immigrants who really built this country into what it is today. It was a good jury. They were very open about their views on some tough topics.

As I will explain more in my chapter on closing arguments, the foundation had been laid for advancing our themes through the conclusion of trial. In closing, I was able to use the jurors' own words to describe the importance of having a safe and calm home. A place of peace and quiet, if that is what you so choose. A place where corporate America does not dictate behavior.

It was also the first trial where I read the jury the inscription on the base of the Statue of Liberty. This really was a case about two immigrants who had come to this country in search of a better life, and now they were in court fighting each other. This is not what makes this country great.

Our themes worked. We received a defense verdict for our clients on all causes of action. Yes, despite all of the missteps along the way, the jury found my clients did not have a duty to investigate after their employee complained in writing of racial harassment and physical violence. It was also okay that they fired the plaintiff right after she lodged a written complaint.

The jury thought a home was different. Our themes clearly worked. An effective theme can have a bigger impact on a trial than any evidence or even the law. And you know who knows this? That's right, plaintiff's counsel. You better have a theme and it must be better than plaintiff's counsel's theme, because she will have one. Your theme must incorporate bigger values, such as justice, country, home, peace, right and wrong. So even when your trial does not go exactly as you plan, but hopefully better than my employment trial, your effective theme will carry the day.

CHAPTER 8

PERSONALIZING THE CORPORATE DEFENDANT

IT WAS JUST ABOUT time. The biggest closing argument of my career was about to begin. The courtroom was packed. It was filled with family and friends of the plaintiff, but mostly it was full of casually dressed plaintiff attorneys. Why were they there? Well, it wasn't to watch me. It was to observe the first-ever president of the famous Gerry Spence Trial Lawyers College not named Gerry Spence. Normally these plaintiffs' lawyers would have to travel to Wyoming and beyond to learn from this lawyer. And he was good alright! Over the course of the trial, it was very clear why lawyers throughout the country paid thousands of dollars every year to learn from him.

What these plaintiffs' lawyers did not realize at the time was that they were watching a bit of pretty important history. It was certainly important to them. In fact, they were about to watch closing arguments in a case that would end up costing plaintiffs' lawyers in California over $4 billion dollars every year!

Yes, this was the *Howell v. Hamilton Meats* case that I ended up arguing years later at the California Supreme Court. But now, as these lawyers filled in the benches behind us, the judge called the courtroom to order. She asked if there was anything else to discuss before she brought the jury in for closing arguments.

Well, I had nothing. For the only time in my career, I had called no expert witnesses at trial, in fact no witnesses at all. I introduced no documentary evidence, or evidence of any kind. When it was our turn to present evidence for our defense, we rested. Nothing. So I was ready to go. In fact, I would have been happy to give closing arguments two weeks earlier, right after opening statements!

But then plaintiff's counsel responded to the judge's question, and I paraphrase:

"Your Honor, before we proceed with closing arguments, I want to object to Mr. Tyson making references to Hamilton Meats & Provisions being a family-owned business. Mr. Tyson told the jury in his opening statement that Mr. Hamilton is a third-generation owner of the company. He went on and on about Hamilton Meats & Provisions being in business in this community for over 50 years. But he never offered any evidence of these things during trial. I object to any further mention of these matters during the defense's closing argument."

Judge: "That is right, Mr. Tyson. You did say all of those things in your opening statement, but you did not introduce any evidence about your client or anything else for that matter. What do you say to that?"

Well, what could I say, they were right! They got us. I had said all of that and more during my opening statement. I was attempting to personalize the corporate client, even if we had no evidence. I was going to try to form a connection between the jury and my corporate client, some way, some how. I was thinking of calling

Mr. Hamilton to testify when I gave my opening statement two weeks earlier, but ultimately his potential favorable testimony did not outweigh the risks of a zealous cross-examination by an extremely skilled plaintiff's lawyer. So what did I say? Exactly what every good, Catholic-school-educated boy should say:

I am sorry your Honor.

But plaintiff's counsel had Mr. Hamilton listed as his first witness for this trial. I thought he was going to call Mr. Hamilton as a witness. But he was never called.

Judge: Well, don't bring up any more stuff about Hamilton Meats being a family-owned business during your closing argument, Mr. Tyson.

And that is how you personalize a corporate defendant when you literally have no evidence! The jury had already heard Hamilton Meats was started by my client's grandfather and was a wonderful, local corporate citizen. What was plaintiff's counsel going to do, stand up and repeat all of the good things I had told the jury about my client but say there was no proof? I would have liked that.

This chapter will address the importance of putting a face on your corporate client and how to do it. But make no mistake, it's imperative the jury knows your client on a personal level in every single trial. No exceptions!

PERSPECTIVE

For a plaintiff, civil litigation is the opportunity to seek compensation for damages incurred. Simply put, it's about money. The plaintiff's attorney will often try to argue on behalf of his or her client for three types of damages: compensatory damages for loss that can be calculated, such as medical bills and loss of earnings; general damages, often referred to as pain and suffering, which is more subjective; and punitive damages, often intended to punish the offending party for grossly negligent behavior. The plaintiff's attorney's job is to seek the highest—not necessarily the most reasonable—compensation for his or her client.

For a defendant, a civil case can literally mean putting their entire livelihood and life's work at risk. As a defense attorney, my duty is to protect my clients by providing the best legal defense available under the law. Sometimes this means proving that my client has zero responsibility. Sometimes this means ensuring my client is only held responsible for damages for which they are actually responsible. And, other times, this means counseling my client to take full responsibility and then arguing for reasonable damages. In all cases, regardless of the circumstances, I take the same approach: responsibility, reasonableness, and common sense. It works!

FACTS VS. FEELINGS

A close colleague referred to civil litigation as a battle between opposing forces where the weapons of choice are facts and feelings. If argued properly, facts often steer the jury in the right direction. But emotions help them decide what to do with those facts.

Consider the following scenario:

John runs a red light while driving the van owned by a local florist company and t-bones Mary's car as it legally travels through a green light. Mary is a single mom who has a steady job as a cashier that pays her $50,000 a year. Mary suffers injuries that require her to miss six months of work and undergo surgery. Her injuries necessitate significant physical therapy to fully recover. The company admits fault and offers to pay all medical bills, lost wages, and future related medical expenses. The company also offers Mary $500,000 for general damages. Mary does not accept the offer and files a civil suit against the company that owns the van John was driving.

At trial, Mary's attorney asks for $5 million in general and punitive damages, in addition to all medical expenses and lost wages.

If I were to tell you that the local florist had a reputation for illegal hiring practices, overcharging its customers, and outsourcing all of its work to non-local workers, would that make you more or less inclined to award Mary more money?

On the other hand, if I were to tell you that the florist has been family owned for three generations, enjoys employing senior citizens, donates flowers to the local high schools for graduation every June, and would go out of business if you awarded the plaintiff $5 million, how would that impact your decision?

WHY WE MUST PERSONALIZE

"You must not allow bias, sympathy, or prejudice to enter into your deliberations."

That is the law. That is one of the basic tenants of any jury trial. Emotion or feelings should have no place in a civil jury trial. We all agree, right? Of course. But is it realistic? Is that what juries do? Do they make decisions like robotic computers based purely on data in and laws applied? Of course not!

The fact is that jurors have feelings and compassion and all types of other emotions, so what should you do? Well, if it's impossible to keep all bias, sympathy, or prejudice out of the courtroom, you might as well have it be in your favor! And who knows this better than anyone? Yes, plaintiff's counsel.

Plaintiff's attorneys understand, respect, and use this knowledge to their benefit. There is an entire part of the legal industry dedicated to offering courses, lectures, and programs that teach plaintiff's attorneys how to connect with their own emotions and how to create the desired emotions in others. They most certainly argue the facts to try and prove responsibility, but also train themselves to draw upon and connect emotionally with jurors to seek out the highest possible award for their clients. This is what they are taught. It is their job and many of them do it very well.

By contrast, most defense attorneys totally neglect the emotional part of the process. Remember, we defense lawyers are rule followers, and the rules say, no emotion. So we follow the rules, present the facts, and argue the law. Since we don't have the burden of proof, this methodical approach often allows the defense to win by knocking out at least one of the three pillars of a typical tort case: liability, causation, or damages.

While this should certainly be pursued as part of the defense's approach, defense counsel and claims professionals should do more. You must make an emotional connection with the jury. You must try to personalize your client, whether the client is a corporation, an LLC, a general partnership, a sole proprietorship, or an individual—even (and especially) when you're admitting liability. Doing so enables jurors to appreciate and understand the value your client provides to society, the impact an unreasonable award would have on them, and how that would affect others.

Telling your client's story may help move the jury to action. It may persuade them. Telling a jury the facts of your case or the law is not persuasive. It does not form a connection with jurors. It does not make someone want to vote for you and your client. It does not address how someone feels. Feelings matter. Feelings are real. They are unavoidable. Feelings, while they should have no place in a courtroom, are there. Who knows this better than anyone? Yes, plaintiff's attorneys.

Lastly, why else must we personal the defendants in every single jury trial? Because it's only fair! Why should the jury know almost every detail about one party to a lawsuit and not the other? That doesn't seem fair, does it? Yet it happens in almost every type of civil trial. The jury hears hours and days of testimony about the plaintiff. The jury will know where this plaintiff was born, where she went to school, how she spent her childhood, what were her dreams and aspirations, who her parents were, who she loved, what she wanted out of life, what she regretted, who she missed, you name it and a plaintiff's attorney will try to share it with a jury.

What does a jury typically know about a defendant? Nothing. Maybe that he owned a truck. Or hired an employee. Or made a product.

But is that who a client really is? Just a faceless, soulless, blank entity? Are clients not corporate citizens contributing something of value to society? Shouldn't a jury know who these clients really are? Isn't it only fair that a jury knows both litigants in a lawsuit, the plaintiff and the defendant? It's your job to do something about it!

THE PROCESS OF PERSONALIZING

We live in a consumer-driven society that runs on business brands. Think about the number of products you use every day. Whether it's the toothpaste you use to brush your teeth, the car you commute in, or the coffee you drink every morning, some type of business creates essentially everything you consume. Yet, I would venture to guess that rarely do you think about who's behind the products you use. It would be unusual for consumers to contemplate the history of the companies that produce those products. The stories of the employees and officers who comprise those businesses, the corporate values and visions, and how such businesses affect or transform the communities in which they operate. But this is exactly the type of information that enables jurors to relate to corporate defendants.

Getting a jury to identify with your corporate client is critical, especially when it comes to damages. Why? Jurors may impose higher damages awards against corporate defendants when they cannot relate to the corporation on a human level. Without that connection, a corporate defendant runs the risk of being viewed as a faceless brand name with a big bank account. Under the California Civil Jury Instruction 104, the defense can ask the judge to instruct the jury that a corporation is "entitled to the same fair and impartial treatment" as a human being. So tell the jury who your "corporate human being" is! Just like the plaintiff's attorney spends hours sharing with the jury who his client is, at least spend a few minutes telling the jury about your client. It's only fair!

HOW DO YOU PERSONALIZE A CORPORATE DEFENDANT?

How do you personalize your client? First, you must do what the best plaintiff's lawyers in America do: They get to know their client. You must do this. And who is your client? Your client is a person, or a group of people. Yes, every company is made up of people. People who have created something of value. These people, employees, have produced a product or a service. Those products or services bring value to others. So while you are defending a corporate client, you are actually defending all of the people who work for that company and all of the people who benefit from what that company provides.

So how do you personalize the corporate defendant? It depends. It depends on what will create the best connection with your jury. It's not the same in every case. You must think about what a jury wants to know. Put yourself in jurors' shoes.

For instance, we had a recent mock trial run by jury consultants in Sacramento for a sexual abuse case against a school district and a criminal teacher. The demand was over $50 million for the terrible things this teacher did to his students. When my partner tried to personalize the school district in this emotionally charged case, it flopped. The jury was not impressed by what we shared about our client. The mock jurors could care less what awards the district had won, how many Nobel prize winners it had produced, what the district's rankings were and its wonderful graduation rates, how many kids went on to achieve advance degrees or invent amazing things. What on earth did any of that have to do with what happened to several little girls left alone with an evil teacher in a darkened classroom?

They were right, of course. None of these accolades or accomplishments mattered. But does that mean you shouldn't personalize a corporate or governmental entity? Do you not try to make a personal connection between your client and the jury? Of course you do. You just change your approach.

Just like the jury instruction says, corporations have the same rights as people. Corporations are people. School districts are people. We had to tell the jury that. This was a terrible, evil, criminal event that affected the lives of many people. Forget how many Rhodes scholars the district had produced; who were the people of the district? In this case, it was the teachers. It was the people who had dedicated their lives to helping and teaching children. These people were betrayed by this evil, criminal teacher. They had sat next to him in their lunchroom, exchanged ideas and best practices. These teachers were devastated by these events. Their lives were changed forever. How could they have not detected such sinister intentions among them? How did they not know such depravity and perversion lived in their midst?

These were real people, with real, raw emotion. We needed to tell their stories too. The human story about the toll this man's crimes had taken on everyone involved. About the loss and betrayal of all. It was real, it was emotional, and it needed to be told. Not run from like most defense attorneys would do, but embraced and shared.

The corporate defendant needs to be humanized. The plaintiff's attorney will seek to prevent this by positioning your client as a greedy entity that places profit over safety. In contrast, the defense attorney's job is to share all the good the company does. You must find the corporate story that's about people. Real people. Real people who have families, who rely upon their job with your company, who are proud of where they work and what they create. Ultimately, a simple question must be asked in order to accomplish this: what do you wish the jury knew about your client? Then it's about using every opportunity to personalize your corporate client throughout the trial--even during the plaintiff's case. The sexual molestation case in Sacramento ultimately settled. But after we developed strategies to humanize the school district, the case settled for an amount significantly less than the $50 million demand.

CORPORATE REPRESENTATIVES

Claims professionals, general counsel, risk managers, and defense counsel must partner to develop the corporate story and provide the jury with a basis to identify with the client. This story should include a corporate representative who is present for every day of trial. The story telling itself will take place during jury selection, opening statement, witness examinations, and closing argument.

Selecting a corporate representative is an important decision because this person will be the face of the client's business. He or she should be present during trial proceedings as much as possible, hopefully every day. This person may never testify, but will serve as a representative in the courtroom and put a face to a defendant company. Of course, defense counsel should make sure this individual has a pleasant demeanor, genuinely cares about the company, and has a vested interest in its future. This person should be selected and prepared to testify well before trial.

Mick Hamilton, president and owner of Hamilton Meats, was the corporate representative in *Howell v. Hamilton Meats*. He was introduced to the jury on the first day of the trial. Mr. Hamilton sat through each and every day of the trial proceedings. It created a lasting impression on the jury. His presence alone demonstrated that he cared about the lawsuit and was invested in the outcome. His presence alone humanized the corporation.

However, I never called Mr. Hamilton to testify. It was a calculated decision. I felt I had been able to introduce the important themes that humanized his company in the eyes of the jury. Mr. Hamilton could have come to the stand and reinforced those themes, reiterated his company's responsibility for the accident, and apologized. But the downside risk was that the plaintiff's attorney would have been able to cross examine him and potentially undercut all of the humanizing efforts I had put in place. The risk simply outweighed the benefit. You will need to do the same type of analysis to decide how you want to personalize your corporate defendant and introduce your themes, with or without testimony from a corporate representative.

VOIR DIRE

Jury selection is the defense's opportunity to weed out prospective jurors who hold anti-corporate sentiments. It's also the defense's first opportunity to begin telling its corporate story.

While typical jury instructions advise jurors they must not "let bias, sympathy, prejudice, or public opinion influence your verdict," the reality is that no one can completely leave their biases at the door when they walk into a courtroom. For this reason, it is crucial to question prospective jurors about their feelings towards corporations, whether they think they should be punished (regardless of whether there is a claim for punitive damages), and whether there are any personal or family experiences that could lead them to view corporations in a negative light.

The questioning also should begin to incorporate background facts about your client's business. This can set the stage for when the full corporate story comes out during trial. You want to begin to frame your client's story as early as possible because the earlier you do so, the more likely the jury will remember the information. By discussing potential voir dire questions in preparation for trial, claims professionals and defense counsel can ensure the insured client's story is presented effectively from the outset.

TRIAL STRATEGY

The best time to tell the full corporate story is during opening statements. Plaintiff's attorneys typically focus on the defendant's conduct during their opening statements, not the actions of the plaintiff. For this reason, defense counsel should use opening statements to reframe the story. Part of reframing the picture presented by plaintiff's counsel involves telling the jury about the history of your corporate client's business and the corporate representative sitting in the courtroom. It also involves telling the jury about the business' mission, its purpose, and what it has done for the community. You want the jury to hear this story from the very beginning, as it will shape the way jurors view the evidence presented during trial.

Depending on the strategy developed by the defense counsel, the claims professional, and the insured client, the defense may not call any corporate client witness for examination. As mentioned, this was the case in *Howell v. Hamilton Meats*. If, however, the defense intends to question a corporate witness, make sure to remind them of the business' history during preparation. During trial, ask them questions about the company's story and contributions to the community. Also, elicit testimony from the witnesses about their personal involvement in the company and what they love about their job. Remind them to be human! Such testimony fosters a connection between the jury and the corporate defendant, further humanizing your client.

Lastly, for all of the reasons I've laid out, don't wait until closing arguments to convey the corporate story. Delaying the story until this point may lessen the impact on the jury. And the defense runs the risk of not being able to tell the tale if counsel doesn't present sufficient evidence to support it during the defense's case in chief. Reiterate the good the corporate client has done for the community and solidify a connection between the jury and the company. If appropriate, tell the jury what an honor it has been to represent the company and how thankful you are for the attendance of the corporate representative.

As demonstrated by the *Howell* verdict, personalizing the corporate client is an essential defense strategy to help reduce potential exposure at trial. It is not about creating a story from thin air or bending truths. In fact, it is quite the opposite. The more genuine and authentic you can be, the better. Putting a face to a company name with your corporate representative and weaving your corporate story throughout trial may defuse juror anger, appear reasonable in your defense arguments, and minimize the likelihood of a runaway jury verdict. Most importantly, it is fair. The jury should know about all parties, not just the plaintiff. It is your duty to tell them!

CHAPTER 9

SLAY THE REPTILE

SPRINGTIME IN NAPA VALLEY. One of the most beautiful places in California. Majestic vineyards dot the countryside for as far as the eye can see. Rolling hills frame beautiful sunsets, with warm air hinting at the summer heat ahead. Hidden away in these acres of vineyards, you will find some of the finest resorts and restaurants in the country. Five-star hotels, outdone only by over-the-top Michelin-star restaurants. Wine tasting tours for every high-end palate you could imagine. If you like fine wine, there may be no better place on earth.

This particular spring, I wasn't at a five-star resort, but rather a chain motel in the city of Napa preparing for trial. No rolling hills or beautiful vineyards, but the motel did offer all the wine and beer you could drink from 5 to 7 p.m. Pretty shocking how much cheap wine tourists can guzzle down at last call after spending all day drinking exquisite wine at some of the fanciest wineries in the world. And, boy, were they loud as we were trying to meet with experts at the buffet to prepare for the next day of trial. But I digress.

My San Francisco partner, Jim Sell, and I were going against the best plaintiff attorney in Sacramento, maybe all of Northern

California. I would say his name, but since I never said it during trial, I'm not starting now. His take-no-prisoners, in-your-face style was very effective. He was seeking over $12 million for his brain-damaged client. We were clearly at fault and it wasn't looking good. It was time to try something new. So we tried the "reverse" Reptile Theory.

In this case, we represented a general contractor who was driving down a two-lane country road. A six-foot-long, hollow white PVC pipe fell from the bed of our client's truck onto the road. It started bouncing down the road and almost went through the plaintiff's front windshield. At trial, our client admitted he was negligent.

The plaintiff was driving her small SUV in the opposite direction around a mountainous bend on the two-lane road. This part of the road was rather treacherous. To her right was a steep cliff, with a several-hundred-foot drop-off. To her left was oncoming traffic and a large rocky embankment. She was facing certain death if she swerved to her right.

As she rounded the curve, she saw a large object moving toward her. She had only a brief moment to react. She braked and swerved to the left to avoid the object. Her SUV collided with the rocky embankment and she sustained a traumatic brain injury, allegedly, and serious back injuries. She underwent a cervical fusion surgery as a result of the collision.

The plaintiff didn't have many favorable choices in her emergency situation. If she drove straight ahead, she risked being killed if the six-foot PVC pipe pierced her front windshield. If she swerved to her right to avoid the pipe, she would certainly fall to her death down the side of the mountain. She really had only one viable option: to brake and turn to her left to cross the road and avoid the pipe. She probably made the right choice.

So we're done? We stipulated to liability in front of the jury. It was our pipe that almost killed her. Do we just argue damages now? Not so fast!

We decided during trial to try the Reptile Theory, but for the defense. Yes, the famous approach used by plaintiff's attorneys across the country to obtain billions of dollars in jury verdicts over the last ten years was going to be our trial strategy. But before I share with you how it turned out, let's explore the Reptile Theory in detail.

WHAT IS THE REPTILE THEORY?

It seems every time you read about a nuclear verdict, there is some reference by the plaintiff's attorney to safety or sending a message. For instance, the defendant corporation did not care about the safety of our community. Or the jury sent a message to this corporation that safety is a priority. The jury was the conscience of the community. Or we are not going to stand for profits over safety.

Look for it the next time you read about a runaway jury verdict. Look for the words "safety," "community," "message," "profits," and "others." What does it mean? Where does this originate? The Reptile Theory has changed the landscape for plaintiff lawyers and their approach to jury trials. You must understand this theory, in detail. If you are already familiar with this approach, you may want to skip ahead to where we discuss how to slay the Reptile.

The Reptile Theory says plaintiff's attorneys should seek to incite fear and anger in jurors. This is described in the book *Reptile: The 2009 Manual of the Plaintiff's Revolution* by David Ball and Don Keenan.[1] The Reptile Theory accompanies the "bible" of the plaintiffs bar, *David Ball on Damages*.[2] The plaintiff's bar

---

1   David Ball and Donald Keenan. *Reptile: The 2009 Manual of the Plaintiff's Revolution.* (New York, NY: Balloon Press, 2009).

2   Ibid. p. 8

considers the Reptile Theory and other new tactics to be a "revolution."[3] Plaintiff's attorneys across the country regularly employ the Reptile Theory in a variety of civil cases, including personal injury, medical malpractice, transportation, construction defect, and other professional liability suits. Plaintiff's attorneys have attributed over $8 billion in verdicts and settlements to the Reptile Theory.[4]

You'd think defense attorneys would have caught on the Reptile Theory by now. Wrong. Even a decade after his book's publication, Ball's Reptile Theory book continues to elude the defense bar. Defense attorneys have published countless articles outlining how to defeat the theory, but its tactics continue to lead to runaway jury verdicts. This chapter focuses not only on how to slay the Reptile, but also how to defeat the Reptile at its own game.

REPTILE TACTICS?

The Reptile Theory says that to succeed at trial, plaintiff's attorneys need to tap into the primitive part of jurors' brains, the part humans share with reptiles, to evoke a fight or flight response: "When the Reptile sees a survival danger, she protects her genes by impelling the juror to protect himself and the community."[5] A juror entrapped by the Reptile Theory not only easily finds liability against the defense, but also tends to award significant damages to the plaintiff. Successful Reptile tactics lead a jury to believe the higher the damages, the higher the likelihood the community will be protected from similar future harmful events.

---

3   https://reptilekeenanball.com

4   Ibid.

5   Ball and Keenan, *Reptile*, 19

A. SAFETY AT ALL COSTS

The science behind the Reptile Theory relies on a basic instinct shared by humans and animals: aversion to danger. In effect, the Reptile Theory is designed to shift the jury's focus from the law—or standard of care—to absolute safety at all costs and total absence of danger.[6] The Reptile Theory's authors draw upon the concept of the "triune brain," first identified by neuroscientist Paul McLean.[7] The reptilian center of the brain controls the body's response to danger and leads us to act out of self-preservation.[8] This epicenter is responsible for keeping us alive.[9] It controls our primal instincts, such as hunger, thirst, sleep, and sexuality. The Reptile brain may also control our procedural memory, such as riding a bike or placing keys in the same place daily.[10]

Research indicates companies can better sell products by tapping into the reptilian brain by relating to consumers' pain points, appealing to their selfishness, using a visual metaphor, and striking an emotional chord with marketing messaging, among other techniques.[11] Others have coined the Reptile brain the "buying brain."[12]

---

6   Robert F. Tyson, "Prevent Runaway Jury Verdicts by Neutralizing the Reptile Theory." claimsjournal.com/news/national/2019/05/10/290858.htm

7   John D. Newman and James C. Harris, "The Scientific Contributions of Paul D. MacLean (1913-2007)," *The Journal of Nervous and Mental Disease*, 197, no. 1 (2009): 3-5.

8   Andreas Comninos, "The Concept of the Triune Brain," https://www.interaction-design.org/literature/article/the-concept-of-the-triune-brain

9   Adam Zemelka, Theory of the Reptilian Brain in Neuromarketing in The Light of Neuroanatomy." *Theranostics of Brain, Spine and Neural Disorders*, 3, no. 3 (2018): 1-2.

10 Andrew E. Budson, "Don't Listen to Your Lizard Brain." Psychology Today (December 2017).

11 Heidi Haskell, "7 Ways to Engage Your Customer's Reptilian Brain," https://www.neurosciencemarketing.com/blog/articles/reptilian-brain-2.htm

12 Zemelka, "Theory of the Reptilian Brain."

Similarly, the Reptile Theory suggests that by tapping into the reptilian center of a juror's brain, she will act out her primitive instinct to protect herself and her community by (1) finding liability against defendants and (2) awarding large damage verdicts to plaintiffs. Jurors entrapped by the Reptile Theory believe, sometimes even subconsciously, the larger the damages award, the higher the likelihood the jury will protect the community from further future harm.

B. REPTILE TRIAL TACTICS

To tap into jurors' "reptile" brains, plaintiff's attorneys frame trial arguments in terms of absolute safety. Plaintiff's counsel will also focus heavily on the defendant's conduct. Counsel will frame the defendant's negligence in terms of the defendant's potential threat to community safety. Plaintiff's counsel will ask jurors to consider three questions when determining whether the defendant's conduct was negligent:

1. How likely was it that the defendant's conduct would hurt someone?

   The Reptile Theory acknowledges freak accidents rarely tap into the reptile brain because no one can prevent random accidents.[13] Accordingly, plaintiff's counsel's mission is to show the defendant's conduct needlessly endangered the community and was highly likely to cause harm.

   Plaintiff's attorneys focus on frequency. The Reptile Theory suggests the higher the frequency of the danger, the higher the level of threat to the community. It follows that a higher rate and degree of risk calls for a company to take a corresponding higher level of safety precautions. Counsel will focus discovery and trial messages beyond the limited

---

13 Ball and Keenan, *Reptile*, 31.

issue of the defendant's conduct in a particular case to the broader question of how frequently the defendant's conduct has caused harm to the community.

2. How much harm could the defendant's conduct cause?

Next, the Reptile Theory implores plaintiff's counsel to focus on the maximum amount of harm the defendant's actions could have caused.[14] The theory acknowledges that most lawyers erroneously focus on the primary cause of the harm or danger in the case at hand. This argument is too limiting for the Reptile. Instead, plaintiff's counsel is told to argue that defendants should choose to conduct themselves based on the maximum amount of foreseeable harm.

3. How much harm could the defendant's conduct cause in other situations?

Finally, plaintiff's counsel employs the Reptile Theory by focusing on how much harm the defendant's conduct could cause in a variety of circumstances. For example, plaintiff's counsel will analogize the danger of a truck driver's decision to drive without enough sleep to that of a school crossing guard's or a surgeon's decision to work without enough sleep. The goal is to show the jury other circumstances in which the defendant's type of behavior is dangerous.

4. Illustrate the "tentacles of danger" and the ability to "meliorate."

Once the jury has been presented with these three questions, the plaintiff has effectively suggested that the defendant's "tentacles of danger extend throughout the community."[15] Effective Reptile tactics must show "the kind

---

14 Ibid, 33.
15 Ibid, 35.

of thing the defendant [did] was a direct threat to everyone in the community."[16]

Ultimately, once the danger to the community is made clear, plaintiff's counsel must empower jurors to wield their power to prevent future harm with their verdict. "Justice enables them to protect" themselves and their community. The panel is the "guardian of the community."[17] The Reptile Theory frames justice in terms of safety, meaning an adverse verdict and a high damage award increases future safety for everyone. Jurors are empowered to "send a message" to the defendant, whose attitude is virtually always depicted as "give danger a pass."[18]

C. JUROR ANGER DRIVES DAMAGES AWARDS

Reptile tactics fuel some of the largest jury verdicts across the country. In almost every closing argument, in cases where a jury awards an astronomical amount of damages, plaintiff's counsel has framed the case in terms of an arbitrary safety rule, asking the jury to serve as the conscience of the community, and empowering them to send a message with their verdict. The greater the award, the louder the jury's message that it will not tolerate this kind of behavior in its community.

While the *Reptile Theory* refers the reader to *Ball on Damages* for arguments to drive large damage awards,[19] its tactics provide the optimal conditions for a jury to award a nuclear verdict. By focusing on the defendant's conduct and fueling jurors' fear, plaintiff's counsel ultimately incites anger over something the defendant did or failed to do. Anger motivates

---

16 Ibid, 36.
17 Ibid, 39.
18 Ibid, 27.
19 Ibid, 8.

a jury to punish the defendant through its verdict, even when punitive damages are not alleged in the case. An angry jury is driven to not only find liability, but also to award the plaintiff a large sum in damages.

REPTILE DISCOVERY TACTICS

To execute Reptile Theory trial tactics, plaintiff's counsel begins to hatch Reptile evidence early in discovery. How so?

A. SAFETY RULES

One of the most important constructs in support of the Reptile Theory is the concept of the "safety rule." A safety rule is a constructed universal principle of how people should behave in certain circumstances. Safety rules focus on preventing danger and preserving safety at all costs. This is, at first blush, easy to agree with. For example, a Reptile safety rule may state, "A doctor must not needlessly endanger a patient."

Safety rules are broad and general. They are absolute, black and white, and apply to a large segment of society. For example, "a coal-mining company is not allowed to turn off the lights while workers are in the mine" is too specific to apply to a diverse jury pool.[20] However, "a company is never allowed to remove a necessary safety measure" is broad enough to resonate with almost everyone. Most jurors care about someone who works for an employer. This safety rule helps connect the danger at issue in the case to jurors' lives.

An effective Reptile safety rule has six characteristics:

1. It must prevent danger.
2. It must protect people in a wide variety of situations, not just someone in the plaintiff's position.

---

20 Ibid, 51.

3. It must be in clear English. Reptiles recoil from legalese and technical jargon. Unclear = unsafe.
4. It must explicitly state what a person must or must not do. "Speeding is dangerous" merely implies a rule. "Drivers must drive at a safe speed" is a rule.
5. The rule must be practical and easy for someone in the defendant's position to have followed.
6. The rule must be one the defendant must agree with—or he'll reveal himself to be stupid, careless, or dishonest for disagreeing.[21]

The last characteristic is the most important for defending against the Reptile. Plaintiff's counsel will focus the deposition line of questioning on a series of questions intended to compel a witness to agree to a universal safety rule—and then ideally corner the witness into affirming that the defense violated the safety rule. A defendant who has agreed to a safety rule and admitted he or she violated it will often have admitted liability on the record.

B. REPTILIAN THEMES
In addition to establishing safety rules, a plaintiff's attorney's primary goal is to develop Reptile themes in discovery that she can then weave throughout the trial. The Reptile Theory provides the following roadmap:

1. Establish general safety rules.
2. Relate general safety rules to specific safety rules.
3. Show the Reptile juror how this harm can happen to him.
4. Emphasize "Safety First, Last, Always."
5. Establish the defendant did not care about safety.

---

21 Ibid, 52-53.

6. Establish the defendant did not care about the person she hurt and does not care now.
7. Establish the defendant learned nothing from what happened.
8. Establish the defendant did not know how to complete the job safely.
9. Expose the defendant as a liar.
10. Show that the defendant did not do her job.
11. Show that the plaintiff did her job.

As discussed below, the defense must shut down the creation of the safety rule from the outset of discovery.

THE REPTILE THEORY HIJACKS THE STANDARD OF CARE

Though many dispute the validity of Reptile Theory science, its effectiveness can't be ignored.[22] Plaintiff's counsel employs these tactics across the country with success, often even over objection by defense counsel.

What is really going on here? How is the Reptile Theory affecting our civil justice system? The impact is more significant than $8 billion in jury verdicts and settlements. Indeed, the successful execution of the Reptile Theory erodes the very foundation of our civil justice system: the "reasonable person" standard of care.

A civilly litigated case is between the parties named in the suit. THIS plaintiff. THIS defendant. THIS set of facts. What would a reasonable person or company have done in THIS circumstance? These questions form the basic standard of care principle and serve as the core of our civil justice system. A jury

---

22 Bill Kanasky, "Debunking and Redefining the Plaintiff Reptile Theory." courtoomsciencesinc.com; Deborah Johnson, "Reptile Theory: Bad Science, Good Results." http://www.high-stakescommunication.com.

uses the reasonable person standard to assess whether a defendant was negligent under the circumstances at hand.

The Reptile Theory coaches plaintiff's attorneys to hijack the standard of care. They will focus on the frequency and severity of potential harm to the community. In effect, the jury will focus beyond THIS plaintiff, THIS defendant, and THIS set of facts. Counsel must "go beyond [the] specific kind of defendant[,]" and spread the "tentacles of danger" beyond the specific harm at issue in the case.[23]

THE REPTILE THEORY IS SPECIFIC:

"Defense standard-of-care claims do not fool the Reptile. When there are two or more ways to achieve the same result, the Reptile allows—demands!—only one level of care: the safest."[24]

While the Reptile Theory claims the law and absolute safety are aligned, the law disagrees.

A. THE REASONABLE PERSON STANDARD OF CARE

To succeed on a negligence cause of action, a plaintiff must show that the defendant failed to use reasonable care to prevent harm to oneself or others.[25] In other words, a plaintiff must prove the defendant had a duty to act as a reasonably prudent company under the circumstances and failed to do so (i.e., "breached" the reasonable standard of care). Negligence claims focus on the "reasonableness" of the defendant's conduct.

The Reptile Theory, however, is designed to redefine and heighten the standard of care in a negligence-based cause of

---

23 Ball and Keenan, *Reptile*, 56, 58.

24 Ibid, 62.

25 CACI 401.

action by effectively turning it into a strict liability standard. To the Reptile, whether the defendant behaved reasonably under the circumstances is irrelevant because someone was harmed. The *only* standard raised is the "safest possible choice."[26] There is no variance allowed for what other reasonably careful people would do under similar circumstances as required in a negligence case.[27] Instead, the Reptile Theory is designed to create strict liability whenever a defendant does not, with the benefit of hindsight, make the "safest possible choice" without regard for other reasonable alternatives.[28] To the Reptile, if the defendant does not make the safest choice available, the defendant is liable when someone is injured.

Negligence actions are not based on strict liability and must not be converted into strict liability actions.[29] Questions, such as whether a defendant "needlessly endangered a [plaintiff]," while seemingly innocuous, are actually designed as the first step in improperly transforming a negligence-based claim into one of strict liability.

Rather than holding the plaintiff to the burden of proof required by law, the Reptile Theory seeks to lessen that burden to proving merely that the defendant did not act in a manner that hindsight reveals may have been the "safest" way possible. This manipulation of the standard of care to create strict liability for negligence actions is contrary to law, and should be precluded at trial.

---

26 Ball and Keenan, *Reptile*, 63.

27 See, *e.g., Mann v. Cracchiolo* (1985) 38 Cal.3d 18, 36; CACI 501.

28 Ball and Keenan, *Reptile*, 63.

29 See *Valentine v. Baxter Healthcare Corp.* (1999) 68 Cal.App.4th 1467, 1484 ["Strict liability is not concerned with the standard of due care or the reasonableness of a [defendant's] conduct"].

HOW TO SLAY THE REPTILE

The defense may use a variety of techniques to stop the Reptile before it begins to slither. The most basic approach requires the defense to spot the Reptile in discovery and prevent the plaintiff's attorney from creating the Reptile safety rule. A more advanced method involves shifting the Reptile's tactics back on the plaintiff—the Reverse Reptile Theory.

A. SPOT THE REPTILE

For the defense to prevent the creation of a Reptile safety rule, it must first spot safety rule tactics. The Reptile Theory provides:

The Safety Rule + Danger = The Reptile.[30]

Defense counsel will know a plaintiff's attorney is hatching Reptile Theory tactics when plaintiff's counsel begins to use "priming" words in discovery: always, never, risk, danger, community, safety or public safety, and needlessly endanger. General Reptile principles guiding plaintiff's counsel's questioning are as follows:

Safety is always the top priority.
Danger is never appropriate.
Protection is always a top priority.
Reducing risk is always a top priority.
Sooner is always better.
More is always better.

Two general safety rule questions focus on persuading a witness to agree that safety is always the top priority and danger is never appropriate. The first type are big-picture safety questions—what the Reptile Theory calls an "umbrella rule," such as:

---

30 Ball and Keenan, *Reptile*, 50.

"Safety is your top priority, correct?" or "You have an obligation to ensure safety, right?" or, "You have a duty to put safety first, correct?"[31]

Umbrella safety rule deposition questions include the following:

- Safety is the top priority of your company, right?
- Is a doctor ever allowed to needlessly endanger a patient?
- Violating a safety rule is never prudent, right?
- A hospital must put patient safety above all else, correct?

The second type of Reptile questions are hypothetical. Plaintiff's counsel often poses these safety questions as: "You would agree ...?" or "Would you agree ...?" or "Isn't it true ...?"

- You would agree with me that ensuring patient safety is your top clinical priority, right?
- Would you agree a company is never allowed to needlessly endanger the community?
- Would you agree a company is never allowed to needlessly endanger its employees?

Plaintiff's counsel may also pose broad, open-ended hypothetical questions to establish a safety rule, such as:

- What would be a safe thing to do when ...?
- Would it be a good idea if ...?

In our experience, corporate representatives are often individuals who sincerely care about their company, clients, patients, and the community. They are also hardworking people

31 Ibid, 55.

who want to be helpful. Such a corporate witness may find it very easy to agree with many of these Reptile questions because their company focuses on doing the right thing. However, to blindly agree with these questions in a deposition may be disastrous for the defense's liability position in the case.

Superficially, plaintiff's Reptile set-up often takes the following form:[32]

Factual/Easy (Agree) – General Safety Rule
Factual/Easy (Agree) – General Safety Rule
Factual/Easy (Agree) – General Danger Rule
Factual/Easy (Agree) – General Danger Rule
Factual/Easy (Agree) – Specific Safety Rule
Factual/Easy (Agree) – Specific Danger Rule
Reptile Question (Safety Rule/Hypothetical)
Case-Specific Fact
Case-Specific Fact
Case-Specific Negligence/Causation ($$$)

The Reptile set-up plays out in the following deposition scenario:[33]

Question 1: You would agree with me that as a property manager, the safety of your tenants is always a top priority? (GENERAL SAFETY RULE: SAFETY IS ALWAYS A TOP PRIORITY.)

Question 2: You would agree that you always do everything you can to ensure the safety of your tenants and your community? (GENERAL SAFETY RULE: MORE IS BETTER.)

---

32 The following questioning framework provided by Elizabeth Skane – SDDL Reptile Theory Presentation (2015).
33 Ibid.

Question 3: You would agree that a property manager should never needlessly endanger their tenants? (GENERAL DANGER RULE: DANGER IS NEVER APPROPRIATE.)

Question 4: You would agree that as part of your effort to protect your community, you ensure that you do everything you can to provide security? (SPECIFIC SAFETY RULE)

Question 5: You would agree that providing onsite security officers is one way to ensure your community is safe? (SPECIFIC SAFETY RULE)

Question 6: You would agree that as a property manager, you have a responsibility to keep gangs out of your community? (SPECIFIC DANGER RULE)

Question 7: You would agree that providing security in your community would have helped keep gang violence out of your community? (REPTILE QUESTION: SAFETY RULE/ HYPOTHETICAL)

Question 8: But you did not provide security, did you? (CASE -SPECIFIC FACT)

Question 9: You did, in fact, know of gang activity in your community? (CASE-SPECIFIC FACT)

Question 10: You would agree that had you provided security services, your community would have been protected against gang violence? (CASE-SPECIFIC NEGLIGENCE/ CAUSATION ($$$))

As demonstrated by this line of questioning, it is simple for plaintiff's counsel to trap an unprepared witness into admitting liability in a deposition. Outside the litigation context, a property manager would love to always ensure the safety of tenants and visitors at his property. It is easy for caring, helpful individuals to agree with these early questions and unknowingly establish a general Reptile safety rule. Agreeing to these initial questions forces the individual to continue agreeing with later set-up questions aimed at trapping the person most knowledgeable from the organization to admit liability. To disagree late in the Reptile questioning contradicts earlier testimony. The Reptile hates hypocrites.[34]

B. DEPOSITION WITNESS TRAINING

The defense against a plaintiff's Reptile tactics begins with robust witness education. Once defense counsel spots the Reptile, counsel must train defense witnesses on these tactics. Preparation of defense witnesses for deposition should move from two-hour meetings to all-day training sessions. Witnesses must understand the Reptile Theory and be prepared to spot priming words and hypothetical question setups. Witnesses must also be prepared for a hostile line of questioning from plaintiff's counsel designed to break down the witness until counsel receives the Reptile answers they need.

Defense counsel must coach the witness to never absolutely agree to hypothetical questions. The witness must not simply answer "yes" or "no." These "yes" or "no" questions are a trap! Instead, the witness should respond with general and clarifying answers, such as:

- Safety is certainly an important goal, yes.
- We strive for safety.

---

34 Ball and Keenan, *Reptile*, 113.

- It depends on the circumstances.
- That is not necessarily true in every situation.
- Not always.
- Sometimes that is true, but not all the time.
- It can be true in certain situations.
- That is not always true.
- That is not how the industry works.
- I would not agree with the way you stated that.

The witness must qualify his or her answers to counsel's questions and explain other inherent risks and considerations. The defense witness may define safety as one of the company's many "core values" rather than the "top priority." A jury will understand and appreciate corporate values. Defining safety as a value guards against the plaintiff's anticipated argument that safety must take top priority in every situation.

Additionally, the defense witness may request specificity of counsel's questions about safety. Seeking clarification will generally throw counsel off-guard and may turn him to a completely different line of questioning. The witness may pose the following questions:

- Safety in what regard? Can you please be more specific?
- Safety is a broad term. Can you be more precise?
- I do not have enough facts to answer your question.
- I need more information to answer the question.
- That is a broad question. To what specific circumstances are you referring?

These deflecting techniques are the first line of defense on the part of defense witnesses in deposition.

Furthermore, even before depositions begin in a case, defense counsel must review the defendant's online presence, including its website, social media, and any press coverage, to ensure the company does not claim "Safety is our top priority!" or refers to itself as "The safest company in America." Plaintiff's counsel will use this material in deposition or later at trial as impeachment evidence. If such content is located, the timing of any amendments may be tricky, especially if the defendant faces a volume of litigation. Nevertheless, the defense must stay ahead of plaintiff's counsel's tactics.

C. OBJECT!

In addition to having a prepared defense witness who provides qualified answers and seeks clarification on ambiguous questions, defense counsel must also object, object, and object again in deposition and trial. Potential defense objections to reptilian questions, particularly in California, may include the following:

- Object as to form
- Lacks foundation
- Vague, ambiguous, and overbroad as to "safety" (and any other relevant terms)
- Assumes facts not in evidence
- Calls for a legal conclusion
- Misstates the applicable legal standard
- Calls for inappropriate, inadmissible, and irrelevant lay opinion testimony
- Argumentative
- Incomplete hypothetical
- [Speaking objection] There are no "rules" and reference to such is improper burden shifting.
- [Speaking objection] "Safe" is not the legal standard.
- [Speaking objection] The question misstates the law.

Defense counsel may make a final objection to any or all of these objections by simply stating, "Reptile Theory." Take every opportunity to call out this improper line of questioning and use it as a chance to educate the judge or jury, should the transcript ever be used as an exhibit to a motion or during trial. Yes, proclaiming "Reptile Theory" is an improper speaking objection, but what is plaintiff's counsel going to do before a judge? Defend her improper line of questioning? Defense counsel must vigorously call a plaintiff's tactics what they are.

D. INSTRUCT THE WITNESS NOT TO ANSWER

If objections don't quell plaintiff's counsel's Reptile questioning, defense counsel should instruct the witness not to answer the question. Reptile Theory questions are improper. The safety rule is not the standard of care. Any hypothetical question based on the safety rule is, therefore, irrelevant.

Furthermore, percipient witnesses cannot answer hypothetical questions without speculating about facts not in evidence. Deposition admonitions explicitly advise the testifying witness not to speculate in his or her answer. In these situations, a witness may simply respond, "I don't know how to answer that question." The witness must be prepared to stand strong in the face of plaintiff's counsel's hostile and repeated questioning. Counsel is extremely motivated to push defense witnesses to the brink in a deposition. Remember, if plaintiff's counsel does not force the defense witness to establish safety rules through Reptile questioning, plaintiff's counsel will have more difficultly establishing liability at trial.

E. TRIAL MOTIONS AND STRATEGY

In addition to robust discovery objections, the defense bar has developed a robust arsenal of trial motions and objections to prevent the Reptile Theory from slithering its way into trial. We have found that the efficacy of defense motions and objections vary from judge to judge. Some California cases have found Reptile Theory arguments are improper at trial.[35]

Before trial, motions in limine focus on educating the judge on the Reptile Theory and argue the tactics should be precluded as a matter of law. Each motion should focus on the specific Reptile arguments the defense anticipates plaintiff's counsel will present at trial. Defense motions in limine request that courts across the country:

1. Preserve the reasonable person standard of care required in negligence cases,
2. Preclude arguments referencing the "community,"
3. Prevent "golden rule" arguments,
4. Prohibit "needlessly endanger" arguments,
5. Restrict plaintiff's counsel from asking the jury to "send a message,"
6. Preclude plaintiff's counsel from telling jurors they are the "conscience of the community,"
7. Prevent plaintiff's counsel from suggesting that even though the plaintiff suffered a minor injury, she "could have been killed" in the accident.[36]

An attorney may not appeal to a juror's self-interest in closing argument.[37] Referencing the "community" is improper because it asks a jury to consider themselves when deciding on the facts

---

35 *Regalado v. Callaghan*, 207 Cal. Rptr. 3d 712 (Ct. App. 2016); Collins v. Union Pac. R. Co., 143 Cal. Rptr. 3d 849, 861 (Ct. App. 2012).

36 Kevin Reynolds and Zachary J. Hermsen. :Defense Techniques for Combating Plaintiff's Reptile Strategy." *Defense Update*, 20, no. 1 (2018).

37 *Cassim v. Allstate Ins.* Co., 94 P.3d 513, 521 (Cal. 2004).

of the case and the verdict, thus impacting the jury's ability to be impartial. Trial by an impartial jury is a fundamental constitutional right for both parties.[38] Inflaming a juror's interest prevents him or her from rendering an impartial verdict. Thus, all references to community harm, asking the jury to serve as the conscience of the community, or empowering the jury to speak on behalf of the community when they render the verdict are inflammatory and improper at trial.

In "golden rule" arguments, attorneys ask the jury to place themselves in the plaintiff's shoes. "Imagine if *your* leg was amputated due to a negligent corporation," or "What amount of damages would *you* expect to receive to compensate *you* for the loss of your loved one?" are both golden rule arguments. Golden rule arguments are prohibited in California and many other jurisdictions.[39] Defense motions in limine argue that plaintiff's counsel imploring the jury to speak on behalf of the "community" is the same as asking the jury to place themselves in the plaintiff's shoes.

Additionally, if plaintiff's counsel begins using Reptile or safety rule terminology in discovery, motions in limine and other briefs may cite specific instances of these tactics to alert the judge to plaintiff's arguments to come. The defense should strongly and persistently object to every Reptile argument and tactic as it comes up to preserve the trial record.

While many of these motions and objections are successful, judges routinely overrule the defense. Some judges agree the Reptile Theory is impermissible in the abstract, but then ultimately permit specific arguments later in a trial. In fact, in a recent trial, we succeeded on a motion in limine to prohibit the use of Reptile Theory arguments in front of the jury. In closing

---

38 *People v. Cissna*, 106 Cal. Rptr. 3d 54, 61 (Ct. App. 2010).

39 See *Loth v. Truck-A-Way Corp.*, 70 Cal. Rptr. 2d 571, 576 (Ct. App. 1998).

argument, plaintiff's counsel continued to reference "community harm" and asked the jury to be the "conscience of the community" with its verdict. I objected and was overruled twice. At a sidebar with the judge, outside the presence of the jury, I referenced the defense motion in limine the judge had granted at the outset of trial to prohibit Reptile Theory tactics. The judge responded, "Well, if this argument is the Reptile Theory, I change my ruling."

Sometimes you have to follow the old adage, if you can't beat 'em, join 'em.

THE REVERSE REPTILE

As I mentioned at the beginning of this chapter, both sides can use the Reptile Theory if the judge allows it. The defense may try to deploy the "Reverse Reptile" on the plaintiff, a co-defendant, or on a party who's not participating in the case (an "empty chair"). The Reverse Reptile is most easily used when there's some element of comparative fault at issue against anyone other than the defendant.

The Reptile Theory acknowledges that the same safety rules apply to both the defense and plaintiff.[40] However, the theory touts that a plaintiff's potential contributory negligence is of limited concern for the jury. A Reptile jury is only concerned with danger to the community at large. Typically, a plaintiff has only hurt himself or herself and is not a danger to the larger community as opposed to the defendant's conduct, which could have hurt anyone at any time. We disagree.

Defense counsel may choose to establish a safety rule that governs a plaintiff's contributory negligence, similar to the plaintiff's efforts to trap the defense in a safety rule. The defense may create rules based on the following presuppositions:

---

40 Ball and Keenan, *Reptile*, 73.

- Employees should follow company policy in the execution of their work duties;
- Consumers should follow manuals and instructions when using a product;
- Patients should follow doctors' instructions after being discharged from medical care;
- Patrons should watch where they are walking in a crowded store;
- Park visitors should follow instructions and warnings on posted signs;
- Drivers should follow the rules of the road.

If the defense successfully entices the plaintiff to establish a safety rule and admit he or she violated that safety rule, establishing contributory negligence becomes more straightforward at trial, also resulting in lower pre-trial settlements.

B. HOW THE REPTILE THEORY WORKED FOR US

Back to our $12 million brain injury case in Napa: The plaintiff was coming around the mountain and our **six-foot-long** white PVC pipe was bouncing in the street toward her windshield. The plaintiff had no choice but to turn to her left to avoid certain death. Or did she? What would the Reptile say? Did the plaintiff put her own safety first? Did she make the safety of the community a priority? Well, she's on the stand explaining why her attorney thinks the case is worth $12 million. Let's ask her:

Q: A double yellow line separated the lanes of traffic on that section of the road, correct?

A: Yes.

Q: What does a double yellow line on the road mean?

A: It means you should not cross the line.

Q: Why is that the law, if you know?
A: For safety.

Q: This is to protect people, so people don't get hurt, right?
A: Yes.

Q: When you're driving, is safety important to you?
A: Yes, of course.

Q: How about the safety of others, is that a priority of yours when you are driving?
A: Absolutely.

Q: You understand if you drive over a double yellow line, you can hurt someone, right?
A: Yes.

Q: In fact, you could even kill someone in a head-on collision, right?
A: Yes.

Q: And you knew there was traffic coming the other way—right at you—that morning because you saw my client's truck, right?
A: Yes, I did.

Q: Fortunately, no one died when you crossed over the double yellow line, right?
A: Correct.

Q: You will agree you had a duty to maintain control of your vehicle at all times during this accident, right?
A: Yes.

Q: But when you saw that piece of plastic, you didn't drive right over it, did you?
A: No.

Q: You also didn't just come to a stop, correct?
A: No, I didn't stop.

Q: No, instead you turned your Jeep into oncoming traffic and lost control of your Jeep, didn't you?
A: I don't think I lost control.

Q: Well, you drove it into an embankment, right?
A: Yes, that's right.

And there is the Reverse Reptile. Through this line of questioning, the plaintiff acknowledged (1) one should follow the rules of the road when driving, (2) people can get hurt when someone does not follow roadway laws, and (3) she didn't follow the rules of the road when she crossed the double yellow line.

Despite our client's clear and admitted liability, the jury found the plaintiff 40 percent at fault for the accident. Yes, even though the plaintiff really had no choice other than driving off a cliff to her death, the jury found her 40 percent at fault. We believe our "reverse reptile" questions substantially helped the jury award the just apportionment of liability and maybe even had an impact on damages. The jury found there was no brain damage. The final verdict to our client was substantially less than the plaintiff's last C.C.P. § 998 offer of compromise, or settlement demand. So, rather than a $12 million award, the best plaintiff's attorney in Northern California owed us money upon the jury's verdict! If you can't beat 'em, join 'em!

CHAPTER 10

SPREAD THE GOOD NEWS

WHAT HAPPENS IN VEGAS, DOESN'T ALWAYS STAY IN VEGAS

There is one point in time when everything changed for me. When everything just clicked. From that day forward, I knew what I was called to do. For me, this moment happened in Las Vegas.

I was thirty-seven years old. I had left a big defense firm and was working out of my home. I had only one client, a nonstandard automobile insurance company. It was usually small accidents with low insurance policy limits. I had a trial fast approaching and it was a big one for them—and for me. This insurance policy was $100,000, but plaintiff's counsel claimed there were no limits and the demand to the jury was over $1 million.

This was a damages-only trial. I had not yet tried a case where we had hurt someone and the only issue was how much were we going to pay. Little did I know at the time I would make a career out of arguing damages. All I knew was I had to win. I only had one client. I also knew I needed help. So I went where everyone goes for spiritual guidance and inspiration, Vegas baby!

I NEEDED GAS

The Defense Research Institute was hosting its annual damages seminar in Las Vegas during the first weekend of March Madness. Vegas was a zoo, with people flooding in for the biggest gambling weekend of the year, bigger than the Super Bowl. I needed advice, and not on gambling. I needed help figuring out how the heck to argue damages. And I got it at this DRI seminar, among thousands of gamblers and I'm sure many hungover lawyers.

The seminar that changed my professional life was given by an amazing Wisconsin trial lawyer named Ric Gas. He turned on a lightbulb in my head that maybe was always there, but I didn't know how to find the switch. Ric Gas showed me.

There was no one particular statement or PowerPoint slide that gave away the secret to arguing damages. It was a mindset, a disposition. Ric Gas essentially told me what I already knew deep inside. There was another side to a plaintiff's story. There was good news to be found. The challenge was to find the good in an otherwise bad event and the subsequent more challenging life for a plaintiff, and tell that story. In that conference room in Las Vegas, when I needed it the most, Ric Gas gave me the voice and confidence I needed to tell that story.

SUPERMAN TO THE RESCUE

Ric Gas, at one point, talked about plaintiff's counsel's use of "day in the life" videos. All defense lawyers sitting in the audience agreed this type of evidence could be very powerful for the plaintiff and damning for the defense. A brief video showing how an injured plaintiff was living after a terrible accident, including all the difficulties of doing daily chores, feeding himself, taking care of personal hygiene, etc., was very visually impactful. Mr. Gas challenged the audience to respond in kind—to do a day in the life video of what a plaintiff's life could look like.

The video he showed, clearly just for effect, was a now-old Super Bowl commercial featuring actor Christopher Reeve. Reeve, who played Superman in the 1980s, had become a quadriplegic from a horseback riding accident. To see a strong, handsome man who literally was Superman to a generation, cut down in his prime and confined to a wheelchair for the rest of his life was truly heart wrenching. This was a tragedy.

In the commercial, Reeve, through the advances of science, was able to get out of his wheelchair, walk across the stage, and receive an innovation award, to the cheers of adoring fans. Seeing the actor who played Superman be able to walk again with the help of science and research was extremely moving and inspiring. It made many people cry when they first saw the commercial. It gave us hope. It gave us what we all wanted for this man—a chance to be himself again.

Ric Gas was obviously trying to inspire us to be creative in our approach to damages. He was showing us a much more positive outlook to an otherwise extremely dire situation.

This changed my career.

Finally, I had a voice. I could be myself. I am a pretty positive person. I do not dwell on the negative and I am very hopeful for all of the good things yet to come. I was able to speak now. Positivity and hope have a place in the courtroom, just like bitterness, negativity, and doom and gloom. I knew what I had to do. I had to go spread the good news. It was truly freeing to me. Ric Gas changed my life!

FOR EVERY WINNER IN VEGAS, THERE ARE MANY ...

So did this seminar change the careers of the hundreds of other defense lawyers sitting in the audience that day? I don't think so. Their reaction to this inspiring presentation was shocking to me at the time, but as the years have passed, not surprising. The lawyers started questioning Mr. Gas about how he would get the Superman TV commercial into evidence. What?

Mr. Gas tried to explain to the defense lawyers, who were focused on the rules of evidence, that this was just an example. It was not real. It was a TV commercial. He was trying to get them to think outside the box. Think about how to tell the jury a compelling story about what the plaintiff's life could be like. He explained that, of course, if you were going to show a video or an animation of how a plaintiff's life could be, it must be supported by expert testimony or other evidence.

While this all made perfect sense to me, and still does, many lawyers sitting near me were shaking their heads. They were in disbelief that any such evidence would ever make it into a trial. And so Mr. Gas did not change everyone's lives that day, but it certainly worked out great for me!

LEAVING LAS VEGAS

I left Las Vegas with money in my pocket and a brand new outlook on what would become one of the most important parts of my career, arguing damages. Both were unexpected and wonderful outcomes from this trip. I took what I learned and not only began a career of arguing non-economic damages honestly, fairly, reasonably, and, most importantly, justly, but I also took it to that pending jury trial.

Plaintiff's counsel had told us during trial he would not accept the $100,000 policy limit. He proceeded to ask the jury for over $1 million. After closing arguments and the jury left to deliberate, the family members of the injured plaintiff were not very happy with me. One sister yelled at me as I was walking out of the courtroom, "How do you live with yourself?"

While that did feel terrible, I understood what had happened. For the first time, the family members realized what we had known all along and what the jury ultimately decided: there was some good news in this plaintiff's life and this was not a million-dollar case. In fact, the jury awarded much less than the $100,000 insurance policy limit. It was, of course, a big win for my client and me. But more importantly, it was a fair and just result for this plaintiff. My career had begun down a new path and I had three days in a smoky hotel in Las Vegas and a phenomenal trial attorney named Ric Gas to thank!

TIME TO DOUBLE DOWN

As I have mentioned several times in this book, connecting with the jury on an emotional level is critical for a just verdict. This is especially true with the doom-and-gloom stories you hear from plaintiff's counsel. Defense lawyers believe plaintiffs have the upper hand when telling an emotional story. Plaintiff's counsel is always trying to convince the jury her client will never, ever get better, or get another job, or recover from the poor advice she received, or whatever wrong is alleged. Literally everything that has gone wrong in the plaintiff's life is related to your client's accident, or termination, or bad advice. This, of course, is rarely the case, but it is up to you to prove it.

Remember, there are two sides to every story. Believe it or not, the defense almost always has the upper hand when it comes to telling a plaintiff's story. That's right—despite all the end-of-the-world, heart-wrenching, negative-Nelly predictions by plaintiff's counsel, you have the opportunity to tell a much more impactful story. You can tell a better story about a plaintiff than even his own attorney.

How can that be? It's because you get to spread the Good News! You get to tell a positive story, filled with hope and promise for a better life. A story based on evidence that the plaintiff will get another job, or improve physically or emotionally, or grow closer to her family, or become stronger, or achieve her dreams and goals, or will be able to overcome all the adversity counsel has droned on and on about over the course of the trial.

And you know what? The jury will like your story better! People want to hear good news. They want to hear about triumph and perseverance and overcoming tragedy.

A TRIAL IS LIKE A COCKTAIL PARTY

Have you ever met someone at a cocktail party and you just cannot get away from them fast enough? Sure, there are many reasons people bug us in social settings: poor manners, incessant talking about themselves, etc. Negativity is one of the biggest reasons we walk away from a casual conversation. Listening to someone whine about their life or about how they've been wronged is the worst.

For example, you meet a woman at a cocktail party who was in a fairly serious car accident a year earlier. You make the mistake of asking how she's doing and she drones on and on. She complains about how miserable her life is. She talks about all the doctors' appointments she has to attend, and all the things she cannot, or will not, do anymore. Each time you try to inject some positivity into the conversation, or point out something good about her situation, she just redirects the conversation to how awful her life has become. Not surprisingly, you look for the quickest excuse to exit the conversation.

Your evening would be much different if this same woman admitted that times have been hard since her accident, but she is focused on getting better. She is going to rehab, trying to exercise, following her doctor's advice, and is enjoying her time at home with family. She is clearly on the road to recovery and is optimistic about her future. Rather than tell this woman you have to go home because the street lights just came on, you might offer to buy her a drink because her story was so uplifting.

Who would you rather speak to? The person who goes on and on about all her problems, doctors' visits, misfortune, and glass-half-empty attitude—or would you gravitate toward the person who has had some bad breaks but is on the mend and is optimistic about her future? Most people would want to talk to the second person, the one who is persevering in the face of adversity.

This is the same in a trial. A jury wants to hear a truthful and positive story. One of hope. An uplifting story, filled with promise, not a bunch of doomsday whining. They want to hear the Good News. The defense must tell this story, supported by evidence, of course. A jury will gravitate to your optimistic version of the plaintiff's life, as opposed to wishing they never came to this darn cocktail party!

The jury wants to know the money they are awarding to an injured or disenfranchised plaintiff is going to be well spent and will have a meaningful and positive impact on her life. You need to show jurors how your number—no matter how much lower it is than the plaintiff's request—will make a positive difference in the plaintiff's life. Your number, and side of the story, will get this plaintiff on the road to recovery and will have a real impact on her life. You must tell the jury the Good News!

THE GOOD NEWS

Many jurors show up for trial thinking two things: First, how do I get out of jury duty? It's a very difficult and time-consuming civic duty. Secondly, once they are sworn in, every juror wants the same thing: they want to find the truth, find out what happened, and do the right thing. Telling a positive story and presenting a plan for the plaintiff to truly get better will empower the jury to return a just verdict consistent with your value of the case.

At Tyson & Mendes, we develop a defense theme around the Good News in every case. This is consistent with our overall themes of responsibility, reasonableness, and common sense. We acknowledge the plaintiff's challenges, but we focus on the good things in a plaintiff's life and the positive road to recovery.

For instance, if the plaintiff's family members testify about how strong of a person she was before the accident, we focus on this strength after the accident. Very often, the accident or other life-changing event did not change the core of who this person is. If the plaintiff was a strong-willed, determined fighter, she is not going to give up for the first time in her life because of this event. A fighter fights. And don't let her lawyer tell you or the jury otherwise. Listen to her family and friends, believe them. Adopt their story, tell their story. If it's the truth, do not let plaintiff's counsel hide it. Shine a light on it and let the jury know you believe in the plaintiff and her strength. Literally tell a jury that: say "I believe the plaintiff's family and friends that she was a strong woman. She is still a strong woman. I believe the plaintiff, I believe her family, and I believe in her. And I believe with the right amount of care and support, the plaintiff will overcome this challenge, just like she has done her entire life."

Sometimes something good, like love, can rise from the ashes of tragedy. Sometimes, but you have to look for it. This can happen with a family of an injured plaintiff. In some cases, as tragic as the event may be, it has actually brought the family closer together. If so, do not run from this, highlight it. Ask the plaintiff and her family about their relationship after the incident. I have had a plaintiff say he never knew how much his wife loved him until she cared for him after his accident. This happens. It is the truth. It is some good news in an otherwise terrible story. Tell it.

We then tie our more positive story and hope for a brighter future to our defense numbers for a reasonable non-economic damages award. A jury would much rather hear a story of hope throughout a six-week trial than a defeated story of how the plaintiff's life is ruined forever. In the end, a reasonable award is not about being able to change the past. It's about providing a fair and effective award for the plantiff's loss, and a path forward on the road to recovery.

For example, assume a young man in his mid-twenties lost his leg from the knee down as a result of a defendant driver's negligence. This is a devastating loss. Undoubtedly, the young man's life is forever altered. But there are two ways to present this story. The plaintiff's attorney, of course, will talk about what the man used to enjoy doing, how his life will never be the same, and about everything he will forever be unable to do. This is real. This man should be fairly compensated for his loss. But the plaintiff's lawyer will ask for an astronomical sum of money that is in no way grounded in this man's actual loss. And they will, of course, never tell the other side of this story.

But there *is* another side to this story, and you must tell it! Your side of the story better come from a place of true compassion and caring for this aggrieved plaintiff. Not a place of being cavalier or dispassionate about another person's plight in life. You must put yourself in the plaintiff's shoes, just like the plaintiff's lawyers talk about doing. Then you must think about what this plaintiff really needs to have a better life. Lastly, go and get this plaintiff that better life—make it happen. Explain how your suggested dollar amount will make this plaintiff whole.

Think to yourself, what would Ric Gas do? How should I get creative? For the plaintiff who lost his leg, explain how his life could still move forward in a healthy and fruitful manner. Research technological advancements for ways to make this young man's life better on a day-to-day basis and into the future. Look to robotics that would allow the young man to swim or play sports—activities he enjoyed before the accident. Look beyond the loss of the limb to ways the plaintiff could continue following his passions and hobbies. To put it bluntly, show more real concern for making this man whole and empowering him to do the things that brought him joy than the plaintiff's own attorney. Plaintiff's counsel will look like he is simply focused on getting his client as much money as possible, not what is fair and reasonable.

THE DEFENSE NUMBER

As I shared in Chapter 3, we give a number in every single jury trial, even when we are seeking a defense verdict. Once defense counsel has shared the Good News, they must tie the positive story to a reasonable defense number in order to avoid a runaway jury verdict.

Like that miserable woman at the cocktail party, plaintiff's counsel generally paints a gloomy picture at trial about their client's struggles and claim it will take millions of dollars to make them whole. Remember, the jury wants to do the right thing. The jury wants to be fair and just. The defense must, therefore, help the jury deliver justice by discussing a reasonable number that will ensure the plaintiff is able to continue on the road to recovery. The defense must explain specifically how the dollar amount will positively impact the plaintiff and help them become whole.

The Good News was critical in a recent $34 million brain injury trial in Marin County, California. My partners, Mina Miserlis and Jim Sell, and I stressed the Good News in the face of an admitted liability and potentially high-value case. A seventy-two-year-old, brain damaged, successful app developer from Silicon Valley sought $34 million in damages for his inability to bring his latest app to market because of a trucking accident caused by our client. Because of his brain damage, the plaintiff had lost the essence of who he was as a person. For over a month, the plaintiff presented experts and evidence to support this substantial financial loss, as well as his physical injuries and his damaged mind. Experts and business partners testified about his lost business opportunities of almost $15 million. His wife testified about how he was just not the same person; this accident changed him.

But like with most cases, there was some Good News to tell. The plaintiff continued to work part time after the accident. We revealed the truth to the jury about how the plaintiff was still enjoying some of his passions and hobbies—work, health, and family. He was still going to the gym every day and was in great shape. He could bench press with sixty-five-pound dumbbells in each hand, at seventy-two years old! The plaintiff's wife testified the accident brought them closer together. They still were able to occasionally travel and spend time with family.

The jury needed to believe that awarding the defense's non-economic damage amount would be fair and just. We explained that $40,000 would reasonably and fairly compensate the plaintiff for his injuries and keep him on the road to recovery. Would awarding the plaintiff $40,000 make him whole? Yes! Would $40,000 allow the plaintiff to follow his passions and hobbies? Yes! This money would allow the plaintiff to travel with his family or it could be saved as a nest egg. It could buy them snowshoeing trips, gym memberships, and puzzle books—all things the plaintiff and his wife enjoyed doing together before the accident and would be able to enjoy again. We simply showed the jury how $40,000 was fair and reasonable and explained why the plaintiff did not need $34 million to accomplish this goal.

We also stressed that if the jury were to award more than the defense's number, the jury would actually be treating the plaintiff unfairly. By awarding more than $40,000, the jury would tell the plaintiff they did not believe he was strong and resilient. A large verdict would tell the plaintiff's family they did not believe the plaintiff was independent and on the road to recovery. It would send the message that the plaintiff would never be able to be an effective steward of his own success and joy.

Of course this a very dangerous argument. It could certainly backfire. The Good News must be grounded in evidence and truth. It must come from a place of sincerity and compassion. What did the plaintiff enjoy doing before the accident? How did the plaintiff contribute to society? How did he previously enjoy spending time with his family and friends? What amount of money would empower him to achieve these things again? You are telling the jury you believe in the plaintiff. You believe his family. You believe the plaintiff will get better. However, you are also telling them what is fair and just. You are giving them a reasonable number that is presented in context and founded in common sense. You are empowering them to do what is right and to feel good about it.

THE VERDICT

When the defense carefully employs these methods, the jury will be well-equipped to do the right thing with their verdict. In this alleged traumatic brain injury, admitted liability trial for $34 million, the jury awarded only $26,000! Yes, even less than the $40,000 we had suggested. The jury believed the Good News we shared with them and they will believe your Good News, too!

Emphasizing the Good News and the Road to Recovery, in an honest and compassionate way, does allow justice to be achieved for a plaintiff. There are two sides to every story, and a jury should consider both sides, not just plaintiff's counsel's negative, doomsday prediction. The jury should be able to consider what good their award can do specifically for a deserving plaintiff, because that is fair and just. Now go and spread the Good News!

CHAPTER 11

VOIR DIRE

A LOT HAS BEEN written about the art and science of jury selection. There are many opinions and dos and don'ts on this subject, but I prefer to keep it very simple: When it comes to avoiding nuclear jury verdicts, my main goal is to have the jury like me more than plaintiff's counsel. Yep, that's it. Why? Because if the jury likes you, they are not going to hurt you. It's that simple.

Can you do it? Of course you can. Will you do it? Maybe, maybe not. I'm sure you have your own ideas about jury selection. As you are preparing for your case, you are thinking about whom you want on your jury. What do you need to learn about these potential jurors to make that decision? What do you want to share with them about your case?

Do you ever stop to think: *How am I going to get these folks to like me?* What exactly are you going to say or do to accomplish this? We are all different. Some of us are funny, some of us are dry, some loud, some quiet, some are the life of the party, others are in the corner. If making friends and trying to be super personable is not your strength, don't worry; you can still do this.

At some point in your life, you must have tried to get someone to like you. Think about that event. Were you trying to get a girl you were crushing on to like you? Or how about the parents of the girl you liked? ("This water is delicious Mrs. Cunningham!") Or some new neighbors or a new boss or new coworkers or a bully, or anyone you have tried to get to like you.

Maybe don't do exactly what you did in those situations (sorry again, Nancy Post, for putting gum in your hair in the seventh grade), but remember those feelings and how hard you were trying to get those folks to like you. Put that same energy into jury selection. Be pleasant and respectful. Be a little self-deprecating if appropriate. Most importantly, smile. Yes, remember to smile when picking a jury. It will help put them and you at ease.

Be polite. Say "please" and "thank you." When someone answers your question, don't move on to the next potential juror or your next question, even if you are rushing. Always say thank you. These people are doing you a favor by responding to your questions. It's not your inalienable right as a lawyer to ask questions of these strangers who are doing their civic duty. "Thank you for sharing," is what I say over and over again during selection. Be grateful and show it when jurors share personal information and experiences with you.

And like at a cocktail party or other social setting, just because you want to know something about someone, or follow up on something they said, doesn't mean you should. Some things are just not for you to know. Very often, a question that would seem awkward and improper in a social setting is also awkward and improper in voir dire. Don't ask that question!

DO NOT MAKE THEM CRY

Even the best trial lawyers can't help themselves sometimes. I was in a trial with a famous young plaintiff's lawyer who has written books about the importance of a "human touch" during jury selection. He made a potential juror cry during his questioning. This juror had shared that she lost a sister. When the plaintiff's lawyer was allowed to start questioning, he asked her to tell the courtroom full of seventy potential jurors about her loss. She started to cry, uncontrollably. Plaintiff's counsel asked for a break for her and a sidebar with the judge. In the judge's chambers, the judge said, "Counsel you better not be asking me to excuse this juror for cause. You are the one who opened the door and made her cry by asking about her loss. This is on you; let's keep on going with jury selection."

He didn't recover. She was too upset and his apologies didn't work. She would have probably been a good, sensitive plaintiff's juror, too. But because he had to know something very personal, information to which he really had no right, he lost her. And of course I didn't leave it alone when I stood up to ask my questions. I told her I was not going to ask her anything personal or anything that would make her feel uncomfortable. You know, like the plaintiff's lawyer just did! (I did not say that part, but it was implied.)

This plaintiff's lawyer had to use a peremptory challenge to excuse a juror from service who would have been great for him. Just because you can ask a question does not mean you should. Remember where you are. Put yourself in the shoes of the potential juror. Fight the urge to know everything, especially if it is personal or sensitive in nature. Making someone cry is the exact opposite of getting them to like you.

INTERACTING WITH JURORS

Lawyers can be very focused on their case and their goals when selecting jurors. It is important to remember that jurors are not adversaries unless you make them adversaries—so don't treat them like it. Do not act like you are entitled to their personal information. Do not try to slip them up. They are not on trial and they are probably more nervous than anyone else, as this process is often new to them. Be cognizant of what you ask a potential juror and how you ask it, because others are likely listening, watching, and judging you. At this point in the process, you are the one on trial. Potential jurors are forming their initial opinions of you.

You want to be appreciative and recognize that jurors do not have a vested interest in your case. In fact, this predisposition forms the premise of the Reptile Theory. Plaintiff's counsel is trying to get the jury to care about the plaintiff. Plaintiff's counsel wants the jury to be thinking about themselves and how they would feel if this had happened to them, or their family, or someone in their community. You want to give them a reason to not identify with the plaintiff's case or have bias for the other side. If there is mutual respect, and a jury finds you genuine, they are more likely to listen attentively, receive your information with an open mind, and ultimately find in your favor if the facts support it. Even if they do not ultimately agree with you, they are far less likely to "hurt" your client with a disparate number.

IS IT WORKING?

So how do you know if the jury likes you more than plaintiff's counsel? There are a couple of ways you can tell. First, the jury will let you know. They will smile at and with you. They will sit up and pay attention when you talk. They may nod their heads, or even shake their heads. They will volunteer when you ask questions. They will talk to you. They will look you in the eyes when you look at them.

Another way you can tell is from the plaintiff's lawyer. Yes, your opponent will react when they realize the jurors are responding to you more favorably than them. They will start to get a little testy after jury selection. Not quite as engaging. There are more extreme examples as well. For instance, in my jury trial against the top plaintiff's lawyer in Northern California, it was pretty obvious after the first day of jury selection that I had gotten under his skin. He said to my law partner, Jim Sell, "And tell your 'game show host' partner to get ready for tomorrow!" Game show host? Really? I mean, I know that was supposed to be a slam of me, but who doesn't like a game show host? The whole purpose of a TV host is to be nice and engaging, and to win over the audience. I will take that insult any day of the week!

How else can you tell if plaintiff's counsel thinks the jury likes you more? In a recent San Diego trial, plaintiff's counsel and I each spent about a half hour asking questions of potential jurors. New potential jurors were seated and it was the plaintiff's lawyer's turn to go again. Plaintiff's counsel stood up and led with, "You will all agree with me that a trial is not a fashion show or a popularity contest, right? It is not about picking your favorite lawyer; it is about evidence and the law. Everyone agree with me?" Wait? A trial is not a popularity contest or a fashion show? You don't think a jury watches everything we wear and everything we do? You don't think people gravitate toward people they like? It was pretty clear to me that plaintiff's counsel didn't like my light blue blazer and purple tie, and he was very concerned the trial might actually be a popularity contest—which he was losing!

Lastly, if you make the effort, getting a jury to like you more than plaintiff's counsel should almost always work. The reason is simple: the good plaintiff lawyers are trying to get the jury angry. That is how they get paid. Getting a jury angry and getting them to like you are two very different things. It's tough to accomplish both. You have the advantage during jury selection; you only have to get the jury to like you. You can do it. And when you do, you will have picked a jury that will never "run away" from you.

NOW WHAT?

"I can't deny the fact that you like me right now; you like me!"
—Sally Field, 1985 Academy Award acceptance speech

So they like you, now what? As with every other aspect of the case you are presenting, you want to advance your themes. Remember, we advance the same three themes in every jury trial. In fact, I advanced these same three themes in my only jury trial where I represented a plaintiff. Your themes of responsibility, reasonableness, and common sense should be introduced and regularly touched on during the jury selection process. Jury selection is the defense's opportunity to identify jurors who are open-minded and attentive, and do not demonstrate significant biases that are contrary to your themes. It's the defense's first opportunity to begin telling its corporate story.

As for themes, ask potential jurors about them. For instance, ask a parent if she ever talks to her kids about the importance of taking responsibility for their actions. Is responsibility an important value for you and your family? Do you think taking responsibility is something that's learned or a trait you are born with? How do you try to teach your children to take responsibility for their actions? Or talk to a potential juror who is in management and ask him if he ever has to talk to any of his employees about taking responsibility for their actions. Ask him to share an example of how he tries to get his employees to take responsibility at work. Why is that important?

Literally ask them about your themes: Who here thinks you have to leave common sense on the steps of the courthouse? There are a lot of rules and laws for you guys to follow, a lot of things you can and cannot do. But do you think you are allowed to apply common sense when you go back in that jury room to deliberate? Of course you're allowed. In fact, it's the law. How about you, Ms. Potential Juror, are you okay with listening to all of the technical evidence and experts and then applying common sense? Thank you for sharing!

How about getting your theme of reasonableness in front of potential jurors? Again, it's not that difficult. Look to the law on reasonableness. It often comes up in jury instructions regarding damages. Talk about it. Talk about how you have a disagreement with plaintiff's counsel as to what is fair and reasonable for the plaintiff. Ask potential jurors if they are comfortable having to decide what is fair and reasonable in this case. If the evidence supports it, can they tell the plaintiff and her lawyer, no, I don't think millions of dollars is reasonable? In the face of what might be emotional testimony and pleas from counsel, can you tell them no if you think their requests are unreasonable?

NO BIAS, UNLESS ...

You have introduced your themes to the jury, and advanced them significantly, so what else do you want to accomplish in voir dire? How about eliminate all bias in the jury pool and have a completely neutral jury? Is this even possible? Nope, it will never happen.

I understand most jury instructions advise jurors they must not "let bias, sympathy, prejudice, or public opinion influence your verdict." But is it reasonable to believe that will happen? Can anyone completely leave their biases at the door when they walk into a courtroom? They can try, but it can be very difficult to leave years of life experiences behind and deliberate as a completely blank slate. So, if you can't completely eliminate biases in a brief voir dire, what should you do? You should try to learn the nature of these preconceived beliefs and, if possible, have them work in your favor.

For this reason, it is crucial to question prospective jurors about their feelings towards the elements and general facts surrounding your case. You, of course, should never argue your case in voir dire, but you should explore if there are any prejudices against your version of the facts. Relevant questions may focus on how jurors feel about large corporations, their take on punishment for accidents (regardless of whether there is a claim for punitive damages), and whether there are any personal or family experiences that could lead them to view corporations in a negative light.

The questioning also should begin to incorporate background information about your client's business or circumstances. This can set the stage for when you begin to humanize your client during trial. You want to begin to frame your client's story as early as possible because the earlier you do, the more likely the jury will remember the information. By discussing potential voir dire questions in preparation for trial, claims professionals and defense counsel can ensure the insured client's story is presented effectively from the outset.

JURY CONSULTANTS

I'm strongly in favor of using jury consultants on many big trials. But this was not always the case. For most of my career, I was not a big fan of jury consultants. I really did not see any value in them. Sure, part of it was because I didn't believe I needed any help picking the best jury for my client. I can sense when people like or dislike me; I do not need anyone sitting with me, whispering who we should take or challenge. I also had some bad experiences with jury consultants. I found them to be a little wishy-washy, and not very science-based. I also had one particularly bad experience.

A few years ago, I asked a jury consultant to join me on a panel at a national conference for risk managers. We were there to advise these risk managers and general counsel how they could help their defense counsel pick a fair jury for corporations. Towards the end of the presentation, after many audience members were complaining about different runaway jury verdicts, my co-presenter, a jury consultant "expert," threw her hands up and said from the stage, "I don't understand these juries anymore, either!" Wait, what? You, the jury expert, don't understand juries anymore? Isn't that what you study every day? Isn't that why you are on this panel as an expert? To explain what is going on with juries? And you and your colleagues are going to help me do my job somehow?

Then everything changed when I met a jury consultant named Mark Calzaretta. Mark started Magna Legal Services many years ago (I unfortunately have no ownership interest in the company!) and has been advising lawyers on case themes, jury selection, trial presentation, and, most importantly to me, scientific juror research. It was clear after meeting Mark that he had elevated his craft to another level. There was science and data and testing to back up his beliefs on the right and wrong jurors for a particular case. It was not just a consultant's feelings about someone; it was tested and true. I have found Mark and his team's profiles of good and bad jurors for our cases to be invaluable.

We have also done a considerable number of mock jury studies in the last few years that have been extremely helpful in a number of ways. Of course you can do mock trials to find out what a jury may think about liability or damages, or both. You can also test themes and some of the methods in this book.

One such example was a recent mock trial we conducted in California. It was a terrible sexual assault on young girls, in the classroom, by their teacher. The most hideous of crimes by the most evil among us, in the most trusted of positions. This teacher was of course in jail for life. The issue in our case was what responsibility did the school district have for this criminal.

These are obviously very difficult cases to defend, even when a client has no idea the crimes were being committed. The facts of this case were so bad, though, that the jury was going to want to hold someone responsible. Even with the perpetrator in jail for life, jurors would know he would never be able to pay a judgment. So the jury would be looking to the employer, at the urging of plaintiff's counsel, of course.

In this all-day mock trial with Magna, we tested our liability defenses and some of our TM Methods, as well. As in every case, we tried to personalize the corporate defendant. In this mock trial exercise, we tried to personalize the school district who obviously had no idea a teacher was doing these awful things to their students. My partner told the history of the school district and listed all of the many successful graduates. She told the mock jurors about all of the achievements their graduates had accomplished over the years. In general, she let the jury know what a wonderful school district this was and all of the many accolades and awards it had received. The district was a great corporate citizen!

What did the mock jurors think? They could care less. They did not understand what any of our client's awards had to do with a teacher molesting his students. It did not make them angry; it just didn't matter. So one take-away could be to not personalize the corporate client in this kind of case.

Wrong.

You must always personalize the corporate client and tell that client's story. But from the feedback we received from the mock jurors, it became clear we had missed a crucial point in implementing this method: we had failed to make it personal. Who really is the school district? Who really is any corporate or governmental entity? Yes, it is the people. People make the place. Tell the story about your people, not a product or a building or an idea or a project or a strategy; make it about people. Get to know your clients and tell their stories.

In this case, we had gotten to know our client, but in the mock trial, we had not really told their story. Their story should have been about their people, which are the teachers. Teachers make the place. Who are our teachers? What do they do? What happened to them during this whole awful ordeal? How did this impact the teachers? How did it make our teachers feel that such evil had been working side-by-side with them, every day, and they had no idea? How could they not have known their co-worker, their friend, was essentially Satan?

Well, our teachers did not know, and when they found out, they were devastated. They love their students. Their students are the reason they do what they do. In fact, our teachers have devoted their lives to helping children. To find out one among them was abusing children, their students, was unimaginable to them. Our teachers were in tears. Their testimony in deposition had been emotional.

Why were our teachers so upset? Because they care. They care about their students. That was our story. Our school district had won a lot of awards and graduated many wonderful students who went on to accomplish amazing things. But our client was really made up of many individuals who care. That was how we needed to personalize our client. We had to show a real jury that we were an entity made up of thousands of people who care. Who come to work every day so our children can have a better day, and a better life. My mom is a retired New York City high school teacher, so I know how wonderful these people are. It was thrilling to be able to personalize this client for a jury.

Jury consultants can be a wonderful asset to a defense team

and we use them regularly. Test your themes with them and get their help with identifying bad and good potential jurors. It will be money well spent.

SELECTING JURORS

You have done your research. You have met with your jury consultant and talked about your ideal jurors. Or you have spoken with your family and friends about your case and what kind of folks might be good jurors for you. You have your ideal juror profile written out or in your head, and now you just have to wait for them to walk in the courtroom. Not quite!

In most instances, voir dire is significantly limited. You will often not have enough time to ask questions of every potential juror, let alone get to know each of them to determine if they fit into your ideal juror mold. So what do you do? I do two things. I try to make an educated guess as to whether they like me, and when short on time, I generalize. Yes, stereotyping is bad, so let me explain in a moment.

First, you want the jury to like you. That is my number one goal—to have them like me more than the plaintiff's attorney. I don't need help knowing whether or not someone likes me, but you may. Some lawyers think everybody likes them. I'm sure you know the type. Although they'd probably disagree, they definitely need a jury consultant!

I don't need a jury consultant to evaluate potential jurors' body language, or whether they're making eye contact with the defense, or smiling appropriately, or not engaged with us. No, I can tell whether people like me or they don't. I always could. Growing up on Staten Island was awesome, but knowing whether certain neighborhood kids liked you or didn't was a pretty useful skill set. When in doubt, I generally err on the side that a person doesn't like me. Just a little insecurity on my part, I guess, but it helps in social settings; it helps in life. Now, I'm not great at knowing why someone likes me or doesn't like me, but I can tell whether they do. And when it comes to selecting a jury, why a potential juror does or doesn't like you doesn't matter. If they don't like you, don't pick them!

So what about stereotyping? It's not politically correct. It can be hurtful. It's often unfair. It is wrong. "Stereotyping" doesn't sound good. It has been defined as a fixed, over-generalized belief about a particular group or class of people. Well, that doesn't sound like something we should be doing.

So don't call it stereotyping and don't do it. But you are going to be forced to make general assessments about some folks you know almost nothing about because you don't have time to get to know them. It's a simple reality of our jury system and the time constraints placed on jury selection.

So what should you be doing? First of all, you cannot discriminate during jury selection. But more than that, it has been my experience that race and gender are not good profile markers or indicators of really anything in a jury pool. In fact, steering in that direction is a distraction that takes you away from what you should be focusing on—relationship building. The profile markers that do matter are the specific thoughts and feelings you engender in prospective jurors based on the questions you ask. Are they easily triggered emotionally? Do they think punitively? Are they analytic in their reasoning?

If I am truly short on time and only have generic information from which to decide, I find that one's profession can help me make an educated guess on some of these key profile markers. Plaintiff's counsel wants emotionally driven jurors. They want artists, caregivers, teachers, writers, creative people, people who have been wronged themselves, and others whom they feel they can manipulate into believing the defense is pure evil. We defense lawyers want analytical, linear-thinking folks who manage people and take responsibility for their actions. These are often engineers, accountants, small business owners, law enforcement, and those in managerial positions. We want people who are detail oriented and often driven to make decisions based on quantifiable analytics. We definitely want people who follow the law.

But, if I had the time, I would throw all of that out the window. I would have the conversations that reveal personalities and real beliefs. I want people who care. People who care about what is fair and just. I want those who appreciate the value of a dollar. I want people who are willing to listen with an open mind. I want people who want to help and do the right thing for all parties involved.

Jury selection is not a science—it is an art. And is a discussion about art ever really over? There is so much more that could be written about jury selection. It might be the most important part of a trial. You only get one chance to make a first impression, and voir dire is your chance. And speaking of trial topics that cannot be adequately covered in one chapter of a book, let's finish this journey with a chapter on closing argument.

CHAPTER 12

CLOSING ARGUMENT

CLOSING ARGUMENT HAS CAUSED me to cry twice. Once before I gave it and once during it. I am not proud of this, but it's an example of how important I think closing argument is for a case. I treat closing argument as if everything, the entire case, winning or losing, all hinge on my closing argument. It's do or die. This is your last, and maybe best, chance to persuade the trier of fact to rule in your client's favor. This is it. Now why would this bring me to tears? I will share that with you in a few pages.

ALL THE WORLD IS A STAGE

It is said that closing argument is the greatest form of theater. Others say jurors have already made up their minds well before the attorneys stand to deliver their closing arguments. While the truth may lie somewhere in the middle, you might as well give the most impactful summation you possibly can.

An entire book could be written on closing argument. I could set forth the exact format you should use for every closing argument, because we do have a proven method for closing argument structure, regardless of the subject matter of the trial. I could share specific techniques for addressing juror anger and emotion. I could show you how to respond to plaintiff's counsel's pleas for sympathy and prejudice, as well as how to address the difficult issues in your case, like money. I could discuss how to share personal stories that will connect with a jury. But, I won't. There is just too much. All that needs to be done in closing argument to avoid a runaway jury verdict can't be discussed in just one chapter. (It could be the subject of my next book.)

Instead, I am going to introduce you to a key component of a closing argument. This technique will allow you to expose your opponent's weaknesses and advance your themes of responsibility, reasonableness, and common sense. I am going to introduce you to "silent witnesses."

WHAT IS A SILENT WITNESS?

A Supreme Court justice once said that "Silent witnesses often testify the loudest."

What that Supreme Court justice meant is that often, the most important evidence in a case is not what is presented in witness testimony or trial exhibits. Rather, sometimes the most compelling evidence is the evidence you never hear or see.

There are all types of silent witnesses, ranging from specific witnesses who did not testify to facts that were not explained. A silent witness could include a longtime primary care physician who was not called to testify by a personal injury plaintiff. Or the number of days the plaintiff went without treating his claimed injuries following the accident. Silent witnesses often testify the loudest because they appeal to a juror's common sense. You are pointing out things the jurors themselves may have been questioning. Silent witnesses tell the jury the story the plaintiff does not want to tell. Silent witnesses yell to the jury, "Here are the facts; do what you know is right."

Simply stated, silent witnesses are the irrefutable facts that empower jurors to set aside complex testimony and apply common sense when rendering a verdict. The use of silent witnesses is a powerful way to advance trial themes and tell a story. Every case has silent witnesses, lots of them. It is up to trial counsel to identify them and tell the jury exactly what each silent witness means during closing argument.

TELL A STORY WITH SILENT WITNESSES

How exactly do you use silent witnesses to persuade a jury to action? Let's use the real life example I mentioned in Chapter 10, the six-week brain injury trial in Marin County, where plaintiff's counsel asked for over $34 million. In the face of a potential multimillion-dollar verdict in this conceded liability case, I stood up in closing argument to paint a complete story for the jury. By highlighting silent witnesses, our closing argument gave us the opportunity to control the final narrative the jury would carry into deliberations.

The trial arose out of a three-vehicle accident that occurred when our client, the construction company's driver, slammed into the plaintiff's vehicle, pushing it forward into another vehicle. The plaintiff, a seventy-two-year-old software programmer, attributed a traumatic brain injury to the accident. He claimed this injury affected his ability to think, work, and ultimately invent and program software. He told the jury his injury prevented him from completing a mobile phone application for famous televangelist, Joel Osteen, which would have resulted in tens of millions of dollars in revenue sharing every year.

Of course, the plaintiff introduced expert testimony at trial to support his brain injury claims while the defense presented expert testimony to refute these claims. After six weeks of technical medical and forensic accounting testimony, I told the jury during closing argument that they did not need the experts to reach a verdict.

Instead, they only needed to rely on their common sense to understand the plaintiff did not sustain a traumatic brain injury or lose millions of dollars of income because of the accident. In appealing to the jury's common sense, I asked them to consider the following silent witnesses we did not hear from at trial:

- The three days the plaintiff waited to receive medical treatment following the accident.
- The fifty-three days the plaintiff waited to complain about his alleged shoulder injury.
- The fifty-nine days the plaintiff waited to report his alleged double vision to any healthcare provider.
- The 480 days the plaintiff went without receiving any treatment for his alleged traumatic brain injury.

What do all of these silent witnesses tell us? What are these silent witnesses screaming out to us? "I'm not hurt!" Right? I mean, we knew this plaintiff sought treatment if he was injured, right? We spent six weeks hearing from all the doctors the plaintiff saw, so we know if he was not feeling well, he went to the doctor. But all of the days with no treatment and no follow-up after the accident were telling us one big thing: "I'm not hurt!"

What other silent witnesses did we have in this case?

The fifteen first responders, emergency care professionals, and other doctors who treated the plaintiff shortly after the accident, but were not called to testify at trial.

What do these fifteen silent witnesses tell us? I can't tell you what they would have said on the stand; that would be improper. We will never know the opinions of the fifteen medical care providers who treated the plaintiff right after this accident. This is some of the most important treatment a person with a brain injury will receive because of the nature of brain injuries. But jurors heard about none of it. How about the plaintiff's primary care physician of over 30 years who treated the plaintiff right after the accident? Never heard from him about how the plaintiff was before and after the accident when he examined him. Why were there no first responders or other emergency care providers testifying in this trial? We may never know. We do know this: the plaintiff has the burden of proof. Silent witnesses often testify the loudest.

Any other silent witnesses in this case?

Yes, twenty more. Can you think of who—or what—they might be? They are the twenty other occasions the plaintiff's attorney worked with the plaintiff's neurologist in the past.

What do these twenty silent witnesses tell us? That this is an unbiased expert who simply opines on the truth? Do these twenty other occasions tell us this is a witness who doesn't care who pays his bills; he's just going to tell the truth? I don't think so. No, these twenty silent witnesses told us this expert was biased, that he was in the plaintiff's attorney's camp. He had been making money off of this attorney's cases for years and hoped to continue doing so for years to come. These twenty silent witnesses tell us this expert had a financial interest in the outcome of this case and if he could keep the plaintiff's attorney happy, he would continue making tens of thousands of dollars, maybe millions of dollars, on cases like this for years to come. I will also tell you this: it is not normal. You did not hear me talking about hiring the same expert over and over again and bringing him into court to convince jurors to find in favor of my client. No, it is wrong. That is not how our judicial system should work, with friends hiring friends to try to convince juries to give them money. It is wrong.

THE LAW SUPPORTS ARGUING SILENT WITNESSES AT TRIAL

There are silent witnesses in every trial. There is always some evidence that does not come into a trial or is not explained or justified. It is up to you to figure out who the silent witnesses are in your case and point them out to the jury. It could be documents that exist but were never shown, it could be a concept or an idea that was not advanced, and, of course, it could be many individuals. You must figure it out and use it to frame your argument. The jury will be listening intently, as they want to know who these silent witnesses are, too.

Once you have listed out the different silent witnesses, an effective way to end this particular section of your argument is to cite the law. In California, you would say, "This is not just a Supreme Court justice who said this about silent witnesses, it is the law. I would like to show you Judicial Council of California Civil Jury Instruction 203, which states a jury, may consider the ability of each party to provide evidence. If a party provided weaker evidence when it could have provided stronger evidence, you may distrust the weaker evidence.' Further, remember who has the burden of proof at trial." (CACI 200)

There it is. You have told a story, advanced a theme—common sense, and it is all supported by the law. When a plaintiff's attorney gets up in rebuttal to finish his closing argument, he will not respond to any of this. How could he? In his effort to attempt to control the narrative and convince the jury he sustained all of the damages he alleged, a plaintiff's attorney will always ignore strong, unfavorable evidence in favor of weaker, more favorable evidence. He will tell his story—he will exaggerate, overreach, and deceive. This can and does result in runaway jury verdicts. If the plaintiff has failed to meet the burden of proof by choosing not to present certain evidence, defense counsel must explain those deficiencies to the jury. It is the job of defense counsel to not just poke holes in the plaintiff's story, but to remind the jury it should not trust weaker evidence in favor of the stronger evidence; it should rely on common sense and the silent witnesses the plaintiff conveniently overlooked.

TEARS FOR FEARS

As I said, I have cried twice regarding closing arguments. One time was just before closing argument. I was on my way to court. Don't ask how I got roped into representing a small business owner acquaintance who sued her insurance agent for not buying the insurance policy she paid him to purchase. But I will say that Catholic guilt is a real thing!

It had been a long battle against a defense lawyer I knew. Their highest offer was $47,000. Our expenses, let alone the hundreds of hours we spent, were more than that. It also was 2008, at the height of the Great Recession. Insurance companies, like most financial institutions, had really tightened their belts and this certainly trickled down to our fifteen-attorney firm at the time. We really, really needed to win this case for our client, and ourselves. But defense counsel was convinced this was a slam-dunk winner and I should be happy to take the $47,000.

The trial had gone well. I thought the jury might be feeling a little bad for my client. She did not get the insurance policy she purchased and ultimately had to declare bankruptcy when she was sued and had no insurance. But she had almost no economic damages. Filing bankruptcy can prevent you from buying a house and it makes getting credit difficult, but no economist could put a damages number on the failure to spend money or get loans. The case was all about damage to our client's reputation and her emotional distress for having to declare bankruptcy.

So I had to get the jury mad. I had to get the jury angry at this insurance agent who took her money, but claimed my client was supposed to be making monthly payments for the policy. I was convinced he was lying. The defendant knew my client had fully paid for her insurance policy and he just didn't bind it with the insurance carrier. He tried to make it very complicated, but he kept her money and she had no policy. But what really were her damages?

After two weeks of trial, I felt everything was riding on my closing argument. I had stayed at the office until four a.m. to finalize my closing. By the time I got home, I got only about one hour of sleep. That was not enough to give the closing of my life. As I was trying to pump myself up in the car ride to court, I realized I was already emotionally drained and exhausted. I could not be an emotional wreck in front of the jury. So while driving alone in my car, I essentially did some of my own Primal Scream Therapy, much like the band Tears For Fears suggests in their song "Shout." I needed to get it all out so I could focus on moving the jury to return a verdict higher than the $47,000 offered.

So what happened? We won, of course! My first and only plaintiff jury trial. The jury awarded my client $1 million, essentially giving her the entire insurance policy she bought, without any real economic damages. The defendant was so overwhelmed by the verdict, he had to go to the emergency room with heart palpitations and missed his punitive damages phase. The total award, including punitive damages, was $1.3 million. A little more than the $47,000 the defense had offered us! I might have shed a tear of joy, too.

There are a lot of takeaways from this experience. The jury felt more than sympathy; they were angry. They listened to our themes, which were the same themes I use in every defense case, and found them to be persuasive. I used silent witnesses in this case as well. Was it as outrageous of a result as the defense lawyer thought? Was it a runaway jury? Do we need to change the whole jury system? Or did the defense get out-lawyered again? I think I know the answer to all of those questions, but let me just say this: As much as I do battle with them, the plaintiff bar does have a tough job. To only get paid if you win is pretty darn stressful. Another reason to defend justice!

I have also shed a tear once during closing argument. It was at the very end of the wrongful death trial of the fifteen-year-old girl and her unborn baby we discussed in Chapter 6. It happened as I mentioned my own daughter with about sixty seconds left in my closing. I was not expecting it, and it was certainly not planned, but it was truly a tragic loss for this mother. This loss really hit home for me, being a father. My voice cracked as I rushed to finish and I needed to quickly wipe my eyes before I could get the last words out.

IN CLOSING

I share these closing argument experiences for several reasons. First, closing arguments do matter. They do have an impact on the jury, a very big impact if done right. Closing argument is your last and best chance to win your trial. Make it count. Make it dramatic. Think about what you would want to hear if you just sat through weeks of testimony and now you had to listen to a defense lawyer. Would you want the defense lawyer to just recite everything you heard for the last several weeks and sprinkle in some boring jury instructions? Or would you want an interesting presentation that moves you to action? Come on, you can do this!

Second, keep it real. Whatever you believe, whatever you feel about your case, say it. Be real. Share with the jury your truth. The truth is, in most cases, that you and your client care. You care about a plaintiff who lost her job, or lost a loved one, or was seriously injured using your product, or whatever the loss may be. Regardless of what your defenses are, show the jury you care. If your last words to the jury are dynamic, persuasive, and caring, you will not be the victim of a nuclear verdict.

Finally, I share these closing argument stories because what we do is hard, really hard. Being a trial lawyer is not easy. It wears on you. You question everything about your case, but also everything about yourself. You will have lots of self-doubt. It is also tempting at times to not fight this battle. To just go through the motions. We defense lawyers get paid either way, win or lose. Why kill yourself over this?

This is why: You are fighting for something bigger than a client or a law or a cause. You are fighting for justice. You are fighting for fairness. And it is under attack every day in courtrooms throughout our great country. Closing argument is your last chance to defend justice for all. You got this!

CONCLUSION

OVER THE LAST 15 years or so, plaintiff attorneys have completely changed how they try cases to a jury. When I first started trying cases, nobody asked the jury for millions of dollars. It was rare that plaintiff's counsel would give much more than a suggestion of a number in closing. They used to think it would be off-putting to a jury, even offensive. Now? If plaintiff's counsel does not ask the jury for a large damages number in voir dire, it is shocking.

What else has changed? Plaintiff attorneys always went for sympathy. Get the jury to feel sorry for their client and you will get paid. Now? It's all about anger. The number one goal of any good plaintiff's lawyer is to get the jury angry at the defense. If they get the jury angry, they will really get a payday.

What else? There never used to be this thing called the "Reptile Theory." It has been a game changer. It has changed the way plaintiff lawyers across the country prepare and try cases. It's creators claim billions of dollars in jury verdicts as a result.

So what are you doing differently in response to all of the changes the plaintiff bar has made? To be blunt, not much. And the plaintiff bar has come up with a strategy that assumes you will continue to do the same thing. We are in meeting after meeting with other defense counsel, claims professionals, general counsel, risk managers, and others, all of whom want to do what they'v been doing since the beginning of time. The defense wants to deny everything and take responsibility for nothing. The defense never wants to give a number, gosh no. And if they do, they never know their number until closing argument, when it is too late. As for the Reptile Theory, everyone files motions complaining about it and trying to prevent plaintiff's counsel from using it. But what really are defense lawyers doing to combat it?

Nuclear verdicts are real. They are becoming bigger and bigger. Runaway jury verdicts are happening every day. So what are you going to do? Are you going to do anything differently?

Do you even care? Do you care about justice? Do you care about fairness, or right and wrong?

I think you do!

DEFENDING JUSTICE FOR ALL

It's time to fight. It's time to stop nuclear verdicts. It's time to take back justice from the plaintiff attorneys who have hijacked it. It's time to do something different. It's time to get out of your comfort zone and stop following the defense herd. Try something creative, something tested and true. Try the methods set forth in this book. Don't try some of them, or part of a method, or only use them sometimes in the right case. Use all of these methods, in all of your cases, all of the time.

Your clients deserve justice. Use these methods and go get it for them. You can do this!

ACKNOWLEDGMENTS

WRITING THIS BOOK HAS BEEN QUITE the journey and I certainly did not do it alone. I have been so blessed to work with hundreds of amazing professionals in our firm and I am forever thankful for their hard work and commitment. While there are many, many people who have supported me over the years and deserve my gratitude, some do stand out.

Professionally, I would like to thank Dan White. Dan was an early mentor and the best defense attorney with whom I ever worked. A consummate professional and brilliant trial lawyer. Also Mike Ripley and Randy Nunn, who gave me a chance and guidance as a very young lawyer and have stuck by me ever since.

I also owe an enormous debt of gratitude to my business coach and consultant, Mort Shaevitz. Dr. Shaevitz has done so many things for me professionally and personally, I cannot name them all. He has given me the voice and confidence to follow my gut in all we are doing to achieve justice for all. Dr. Shaevitz, "The Lawyer Whisperer." Thank you for pushing me to write this book!

I would like to thank my law partners for helping me develop many of the Tyson & Mendes Methods I discuss in this book and also for being open to allowing me to publish the first book ever written for the defense on how to argue damages and avoid runaway jury verdicts. A special thanks to those I have tried cases with, especially Mina Miserlis, Jim Sell, Kristi Blackwell, Dan Fallon, and Jake Felderman. Some of the best memories of my career! And a special thank you to Susan Oliver, who was my good friend first and my amazing partner second.

And thank you to all of the attorneys who helped with the writing of this book, especially Cayce Lynch who, as our administrative partner, is amazing; Jessica Heppenstall, Reece Roman, Morgan Van Buren, Emily Straub, Kelly Denham, Pari Granum, Kate Besch, Kyle Pederson, and soon-to-be attorney Tina Mihelich. Your commitment to justice and the TM Methods is greatly appreciated.

One last professional thank you to all of our clients. Without you and your trust in us trying these different methods to fight for justice, none of this would have been possible. Without my clients, I would never have become a trial attorney. I never forget that. Thank you!

Personally, I would like to thank my longtime friend Father John Stack from Villanova University. From the first day we met on a basketball court thirty-seven years ago on campus, you have challenged me to be a better person. It has been exhausting at times, but full of laughs. Thank you Father.

Behind every great man is a great .... I couldn't resist a jab at my partner and best friend, Pat Mendes. It has been quite the ride, my friend, since two Catholic school mama's boys met in a San Diego law firm. Being partners with your best friend has its challenges for sure, but it has certainly been an awesome journey together! Thank you.

My family. Three wonderful children: Faith, Mary, and Bobby, and my beautiful wife, Jenny. I could go on and on about all the happiness and love you have brought into my life. You guys are the reason for all of this and the joy of my life. Thank you!

To my sister Denise Tyson who wanted to be remembered in my book: Hello Denise!

Finally, my parents Bob and Diane. There is no greater influence on who I am today than the two of you. In everything you have said and done, you have inspired me to do more and be more. I am forever grateful for all of your sacrifices. I am so blessed to still have you both in my life. I love you and thank you!

Let's go!

INDEX